JEFFREY A. GILL

The Last Will Be First

The Last Will Be First

by
John MacArthur, Jr.

WORD OF GRACE COMMUNICATIONS
P.O. Box 4000
Panorama City, CA 91412

All Scripture quotations, unless noted otherwise, are from the *New Scofield
Reference Bible*, King James Version. Copyright © 1967 by Oxford Univer-
sity Press, Inc. Reprinted by permission.

Library of Congress Cataloging in Publication Data

MacArthur, John F.
    The last will be first.

    (John MacArthur's Bible studies)
    Includes index.
    1. Bible. N.T. Matthew—Criticism, interpretation,
etc. I. Title. II. Series: MacArthur, John F. Bible
studies.
BS2575.2.M25   1987   226'.206   86-28476
ISBN 0-8024-5347-3

1 2 3 4 5 6 7 Printing/LC/Year 91 90 89 88 87

Printed in the United States of America

Contents

These Bible studies are taken from messages delivered by Pastor-Teacher John MacArthur, Jr., at Grace Community Church in Panorama City, California. These messages have been combined into a 6-tape album entitled *The Last Will Be First*. You may purchase this series either in an attractive vinyl cassette album or as individual cassettes. To purchase these tapes, request the album *The Last Will Be First*, or ask for the tapes by their individual GC numbers. Please consult the current price list; then, send your order, making your check payable to:

WORD OF GRACE COMMUNICATIONS
P.O. Box 4000
Panorama City, CA 91412

Or call the following number:
818-982-7000

1

How to Obtain Eternal Life

Outline

Introduction
A. The Purpose of Evangelism
B. The Methods of Evangelism
   1. Of Jesus
   2. Of contemporary evangelism

Lesson
 I. Know What You Want (v. 16)
    A. What the Ruler Had
    B. What the Ruler Lacked
       1. Eternal life defined
       2. Eternal life desired
 II. Have a Deep-Felt Need (v. 16)
    A. The Lack of Desperation
    B. The Urgency of Desperation
III. Seek Diligently (v. 16)
    A. The Ruler's Self-Centered Attitude
    B. The Ruler's Humble Approach
IV. Come to the Right Source (v. 16)
    A. The Counterfeits of Satan
    B. The Cornerstone of Christ
    C. The Conclusion of the Ruler
       1. About the morality of Christ
       2. About the deity of Christ
 V. Ask the Right Question (v. 16)
VI. Confess Your Sinfulness (vv. 17-20)
    A. The Lord's Command (vv. 17-19)
       1. The requirement for salvation (v. 17)
          a) An incomplete understanding
          b) An insensitive perspective

Introduction

During a flight I took some time ago, a young man sitting next to me introduced himself and said, "Sir, you wouldn't know how I could have a relationship with Jesus Christ, would you?" Now that sort of incident doesn't happen often! I was reading my Bible, which prompted him to ask the question. He seemed ready and eager to be saved. I said, "You simply believe in the Lord Jesus Christ and accept Him as your Savior." He said, "I'd like to do that." So we prayed together. I was excited about what happened but was later unsuccessful in my attempts to follow up his commitment. I have since discovered that he has had no continuing interest in the things of Christ.

You may have led someone to Christ who then showed no change in his life. If you've ever struggled to understand why that happens, I believe you'll find the answer in this lesson. I didn't fully understand why it happens until I understood Matthew 19:16-22. Its message can be summed up by the Lord's words in Luke 14:33, "Whosoever he is of you that forsaketh not all that he hath, cannot be my disciple." That is a straightforward truth. Salvation is not necessarily for people who pray a prayer or think they need Jesus Christ; it is for people who forsake everything. They must be willing to abandon everything for genuine salvation.

Let's look at the text: "Behold, one came and said unto him, Good Master, what good thing shall I do, that I may have eternal life? And he said unto him, Why callest thou me good? There is none good but one, that is, God; but if thou wilt enter into life, keep the commandments. He saith unto him, Which? Jesus said, Thou shalt do no murder, Thou shalt not commit adultery, Thou shalt not steal, Thou shalt not bear false witness, Honor thy father and thy mother; and, Thou shalt love thy neighbor as thyself. The young man saith unto him, All these things have I kept from my youth up. What lack I yet? Jesus said unto him, If thou wilt be perfect, go and sell what thou hast, and give to the poor, and thou shalt have treasure in heaven; and come and follow me. But when the young man heard that saying, he went away sorrowful; for he had great possessions." Jesus gave the man a test: he had to choose between his possessions and Jesus Christ. But because he was unwilling to forsake all, he never could be a disciple of Christ.

A. The Purpose of Evangelism

The young man in Matthew 19:16 wants to know how he can obtain eternal life. The phrase "eternal life" is used about fifty times in Scripture. The heart of all evangelism is to get people to seek and then receive eternal life. John 3:16 says, "For God so loved the world, that he gave his only begotten Son, that whosoever believeth in him should not perish, but have everlasting life."

Much of evangelism involves getting people to the point that the young man of Matthew 19 had already reached. Many of us believe that when we get someone to say, "What do I need to do to inherit eternal life?" all we have to do is say, "Believe; sign the card; raise your hand; walk the aisle." When the young man asked Jesus the right question, he didn't need to be prompted to respond to the gospel; he was already interested—just like the young man I encountered on the plane. The Lord was asked the same question on several occasions in the New Testament (e.g., John 6:28).

B. The Methods of Evangelism

The young man in Matthew 19 is one of the hottest evangelistic prospects in the gospels. He was ready. But amazingly, he went away without ever receiving eternal life.

The reason is simple: he was not willing to forsake everything.

1. Of Jesus

Jesus set up an insurmountable barrier for the young man. Instead of getting him to make a decision, Jesus stopped him. Now what kind of evangelism is that? Jesus would have flunked the evangelism seminar! He didn't know how to sign the guy up. He missed out on a hot prospect. You certainly don't want to lose someone like him!

2. Of contemporary evangelism

Many contemporary modes of evangelism are not biblical. Our present-day mass evangelism, with its decision statistics and its aisle-walking emphasis, is leading some people into the delusion that they're saved when they're not. That's why we must go to Matthew 19:16-22 for its important instruction.

To understand why this young man turned away from eternal life, let's ask a question similar to his: How does one obtain eternal life?

Lesson

I. KNOW WHAT YOU WANT (v. 16)

The man came to Jesus wanting to obtain eternal life. He knew what he wanted, and that's where everyone has to start. You've got to know what it is you seek before you can seek it. This man wanted eternal life because he knew he didn't have it.

A. What the Ruler Had

Matthew tells us the man was young (v. 20) and rich (v. 22). Luke tells us in Luke 18:18 that he was a ruler (Gk., *archē*). I think he was a ruler of a synagogue (cf. Matt. 9:18; Luke 8:41), which was extremely rare for a young man. As a Jewish religious leader, he would probably have been devout, honest (in terms of his relationship to Judaism), wealthy, prominent, and influential. In terms of his cultural and religious environment, he had everything. I think that's why Matthew says "And, behold" in verse 16. In our vernacular, that exclamation could be translated as, "Can you believe this?" It was amazing that a man of his stature would come to Jesus and admit he didn't have eternal life.

B. What the Ruler Lacked

The man had not found the reality that could put his soul to rest. He lacked a confident, permanent peace, joy, and hope. He came to Jesus on the grounds of felt need. There was restlessness and anxiety in his heart. There was a sense of unfulfillment. And he knew what was missing—eternal life. But how did he know?

1. Eternal life defined

The Jews understood the concept of eternal life. Since life is the ability to respond to the environment, eternal life is the ability to respond to the divine environment—forever. We respond to the life of Christ. When we're saved, we enter into the heavenlies (Eph. 1:3). Our citizenship takes on an unending divine character. We come alive to God. Eternal life is more a *quality* of existence than a *quantity* of existence. When I believed, I became sensitive to God; I could respond to Him. Before I was saved, I was dead in sin—totally unresponsive to the divine environment. When I became a Christian, I became capable of responding to the divine environment.

2. Eternal life desired

The young man knew he did not have the ability to respond fully to the divine environment. He wasn't sensing God's love, rest, peace, hope, and joy—the things that give the security of belonging to God. He knew he didn't possess the divine life. He knew he didn't have the life of God in his soul. He knew he didn't walk with God or commune with Him. He had gone beyond the Pharisees, who were content with their own musings and prayers to themselves. He knew he was missing out on a quality of life. It is important to understand that eternal life is more than just living forever; it is the ability to respond to God.

Older and Older

The idea that eternal life merely equals length of life is reflected in the Greek myth about Aurora, the goddess of the dawn. She fell in love with Tithonus, a mortal youth. She didn't want him to die, so she went to Zeus, the head of the Greek gods. She asked that Tithonus never die, and Zeus granted her request. But Aurora forgot to ask that he would stay young forever. So Tithonus lived forever, but he became older and older until life was a horrible punishment. That's not eternal life in the biblical sense. Eternal life is the process of unending communion with the living God.

The rich young ruler knew what he wanted. When we preach or evangelize, our efforts need to be aimed at getting people to understand that they should want eternal life.

II. HAVE A DEEP-FELT NEED (v. 16)

A. The Lack of Desperation

There are people who know they don't have eternal life but don't feel any need for it. They know they're not alive to God, and they don't care to be. They know they don't sense the divine dimension or have security in the life to come, but they really aren't interested. They're not desperate enough to want what they don't have. The young man was. He knew what he wanted and deeply felt the need for it.

B. The Urgency of Desperation

There is an urgency in the young man's question: "Good Master, what good thing shall I do, that I may have eternal life?" (v. 16). After claiming he had kept all the commandments Jesus named, the man said, "What lack I yet?" (v. 20). I sense frustration, unfulfillment, and anxiety in that question. His life had been one great effort at being religious, but there was something missing.

This man was a great prospect. He knew he didn't have eternal life. He wanted it badly because he had an emptiness in his life. Certainly he had lived an exemplary life. He had avoided external sins. He was moral and religious. He had conformed to the standards of his religion. He was a leader in the eyes of the people. Yet he was unsatisfied because he knew he lacked eternal life.

III. SEEK DILIGENTLY (v. 16)

Jesus waited for the man to come to Him. How can we know the young man was a diligent seeker? All Matthew 19:16 says is "one came." But the parallel passage in Mark 10:17 says, "There came one running." There is urgency in his approach. There was frustration in his heart. He was a religious man with integrity. I think he wanted the peace and joy that come with knowing God. Those elements were missing in his life.

A. The Ruler's Self-Centered Attitude

There is one thing about this man that must be pointed out: he was self-centered. He came to Jesus to satisfy the need of his heart. That's not a wrong motive; it's just imcomplete.

B. The Ruler's Humble Approach

Mark 10:17 indicates that the Lord was walking down a road, and no doubt a crowd had gathered around Him. The young man ran into that crowd. If he indeed was a ruler of the synagogue, they surely knew him, yet he wasn't embarrassed by his public confession that he lacked eternal life. That was an extraordinary confession from a person of his stature.

Mark adds that the man got down on his knees before Jesus. That was a position of humility. He was a man of great integrity, who was serious, motivated, and anxious. He wanted eternal life so badly and sought it so diligently that he didn't mind losing face with all the people who already thought he was a spiritual giant.

Now you would think that this was a great opportunity for him to become saved. He was ready for salvation. It would have been great to have a man of his stature accept Christ's teaching. He seemed to be a perfect prospect.

IV. COME TO THE RIGHT SOURCE (v. 16)

A. The Counterfeits of Satan

Many people are looking for eternal life in the wrong places. Satan has counterfeit religions all over the earth. Those people won't find eternal life, but many keep diligently seeking. However, this man came to the right source.

B. The Cornerstone of Christ

First John 5:11 says, "This is the record, that God hath given to us eternal life, and this life is in his Son." Verse 20 says Jesus Christ "is the true God, and eternal life." Jesus is not just the source of eternal life; He is eternal life itself.

C. The Conclusion of the Ruler

1. About the morality of Christ

The young man had probably heard of the power of Jesus. No doubt he had heard of His teaching, because he said to Him, "Good Master [Gk., *didaskale*, "teacher"]." He acknowledged Jesus as a teacher of divine truth. Mark 10:17 and Luke 18:18 indicate that he called Jesus "good." (That word was added in the King James Version in Matthew, but it wasn't included in the original manuscripts.) There are two Greek words for "good." *Kalos* refers to what is good in form, or good on the outside. The word used in Mark and Luke is *agathos*, which means "good on the inside," "good morally," or "good in essence." He acknowledged Jesus as a morally good person. He knew Jesus taught divine truth and was sure He knew the secret of obtaining eternal life.

2. About the deity of Christ

> I don't think the man thought Jesus was God. I don't
> even think he particularly thought of Him as the Mes-
> siah, because he referred to Him as a morally good
> teacher. I do think he was so struck with the power of
> Jesus' teaching and the power of His life that he
> thought Jesus knew the secret of eternal life and how
> he might receive it.

Although the man didn't know who Jesus was in the fullest
sense, he certainly came to the right source. Acts 4:12 says,
"Neither is there salvation in any other; for there is no other
name under heaven given among men, whereby we must be
saved."

V. ASK THE RIGHT QUESTION (v. 16)

Many people have discredited the man for asking, "What
good thing shall I do?" thinking he was asking a works-oriented question. Certainly he was works-oriented—he was
raised in the Pharisaic system of tradition. He was trained to
believe that you did religious things to gain divine favor. But I
still think his question was a fair one. There's nothing in the
text to indicate that he was emphasizing one specific work.
The fact is, you *do* have to do something to receive eternal life:
you have to believe in Christ. Your will has to be involved.
There has to be a response. He didn't say, "How can I be
more religious?" "How can I be more moral?" or "How can I
develop more self-respect?" He said, "I want eternal life.
What do I do to receive it?" It was not a question aimed at trying to trap Jesus. He was not trying to offer his self-righteousness as a solution to gain eternal life; he simply asked an
honest question.

The man's question is reminiscent of the one the people ask
Jesus in John 6:28: "What shall we do, that we might work the
works of God?" Now that was a works-oriented question. Jesus responded, "This is the work of God, that ye believe on
him whom he hath sent" (v. 29). We must act in faith, activat-
ing our will to trust in Christ. The man also asked, "What *good*
thing?" (emphasis added). He knew he had to do something
genuinely good.

VI. CONFESS YOUR SINFULNESS (vv. 17-20)

Jesus' answer is amazing. A contemporary evangelical might say, "Just believe. Jesus died for you and rose again. If you believe that, pray and ask Jesus into your heart. Confess Him as your Savior, and you'll be saved." But Jesus didn't do that. He put up a wall and drew the man to a sudden stop.

A. The Lord's Command (vv. 17-19)

1. The requirement for salvation (v. 17)

"He said unto him, Why callest thou me good? There is none good but one, that is, God; but if thou wilt enter into life, keep the commandments."

Jesus was saying, "Why are you asking Me what good thing you have to do? Do you think I've got some secret no one else knows about? There's none good but God, and you know what He said. So if you want life, then keep the commandments. You know what they are; you don't need to ask Me." The man knew the good things that were written in the law of God; he just needed to do them. God alone is good. It is in His goodness that He has revealed His will. The man knew the revelation of God and the law of God. Jesus didn't add anything to it, so all the man had to do was keep it all.

a) An incomplete understanding

There was something missing in the man's approach. He came to Jesus seeking salvation based on his felt need. He was experiencing anxiety and frustration, and he wanted to experience joy, love, peace, and hope. Yet that is not a good enough reason to come to Christ. If we offer people happiness, joy, and peace, we'll have a great response. All we would need to do is find all those who are psychologically incomplete. If we can offer people the panaceas to their anxieties through Jesus, they'll take Him right away. But that is not a complete understanding of salvation.

b) An insensitive perspective

Jesus told the man that the one thing he hadn't done was something he already knew about, and that was to keep all the commandments God had revealed in His Word. Now of course no one can do that, and that's exactly what Jesus wanted the rich young ruler to realize. The man's problem was his sin. It hadn't even been mentioned. He had no sense of offending a holy God. His desire for eternal life was wrapped up in his own anxieties and needs. He failed to consider that his life was an affront to an infinitely holy God. Such a realization is necessary in understanding the truth of salvation.

c) An imperative confrontation

The one good thing Jesus told the man he had to do was keep the law of God. There was nothing Jesus could add. God is good and has revealed His good will, which is His law, and which must be kept. Could you be saved if you kept the commandments? Yes, but you can't keep them. The young man had to be confronted with the fact that he had violated God.

(1) Necessary confession

You cannot bring people to Jesus Christ simply on the basis of psychological needs and anxieties or the lack of peace, hope, joy, or happiness. They must understand that salvation is for people who want to turn away from the things of this life and turn to God. It is for those who see they have lived in violation and rebellion against holy God. They have to want to turn around, confess their sin, and affirm their commitment to live for His glory. All the young man felt was a personal need. He felt anxiety. And he felt there was something lacking in his life. But that is not enough.

Our Lord shifted the focus from the young man to God. He tried to show the young man that the real problem in his life was what he was doing to offend a holy God. When He said, "Keep the commandments," He held up the man's life against the divine standard so he might see that he came up short.

As I look back on the time I spent talking to the young man on the plane, I realize that I took him at face value. I led him to Christ for his psychological needs without making him understand that he needed to receive Christ to deal with his sin. When you share the gospel with others, make sure they understand the full nature of their sinfulness—that it violates the holy law of God. All evangelism must take the imperfect sinner and place him up against the perfect law of God so he can see his deficiency. That's an essential element. Evangelism that deals only with men's needs, feelings, and problems lacks true balance. That is why churches are jammed full of people who aren't really saved—because they sought and gained psychological affirmation and not transactional redemption. Why do you think Paul spends the first three chapters of Romans affirming the sinfulness of man before getting to the subject of salvation? Because man's sin is the issue.

(2) Necessary remorse

The rich young ruler had no sense of offending God. He had no remorse. I believe remorse needs to precede salvation (cf. Matt. 5:4). A man must manifest the attitudes that Christ presents in the Beatitudes. He needs to beg God for forgiveness. He needs a sense of meekness. He needs to manifest a mournful heart that is overwhelmed by his sin. But the ruler didn't have that. He wanted his psychological needs met, period. I don't see remorse over sin in this passage at all. I don't see the man saddened that he had offended God. And I don't see him even

18

aware of his sin. You must not approach people on the basis that Christ will meet their psychological needs.

This may sound like heresy, but did you know that God does *not* have a wonderful plan for an unbeliever's life? He has a horrible plan for those who don't know Christ. When we approach people, we must approach the problem of sin. The Old Testament says, "God is angry with the wicked every day" (Ps. 7:11). A good, holy, and pure God cannot tolerate evil. So Jesus affirmed what must always be affirmed—there is a divine law that must be kept. If you violate that law, you're under the judgment of God.

Christ set up a barrier for the young man by explaining that his reasons for wanting eternal life were incomplete. He needed to see that he was living in violation of holy God and be willing to change.

2. The recitation of the commands (vv. 18-19)

The young man responded to Jesus' command by saying, "Which?" He wanted to know which laws he needed to keep. So the Lord gave him five of the last of the Ten Commandments: "Thou shalt not murder, Thou shalt not commit adultery, Thou shalt not steal, Thou shalt not bear false witness, honor thy father and thy mother" (vv. 18-19). Then He adds, "Thou shalt love thy neighbor as thyself," which is from the book of Leviticus (19:18). The Ten Commandments are divided into two parts. The first four deal with man's relationship to God; the second six deal with man's relationship to man. Jesus gives the young man the second group, which are easier to keep, relatively speaking. You know you haven't loved God the way you should and that you haven't always been totally honest before Him, but at least you might say, "I never killed anyone. I never stole from anyone. I never committed adultery with anyone. I never deliberately lied to anyone. And I've always tried to honor my father and mother." So

Christ gives the young man the benefit of the doubt and gives him the easier group of the impossible. Then He adds one command at the end just to make it more difficult: "Thou shalt love thy neighbor as thyself" (v. 19). Jesus put the man's life against the Ten Commandments, including Leviticus 19:18, so that he might understand he was violating God's law. Sin against the law of God is the issue in salvation, not psychological need or religious desire.

You can't preach grace until you preach law because no one can understand what grace means unless he understands what the law requires. No one can understand mercy unless he understands guilt. You cannot preach a gospel of grace unless you've preached a message of law. And that's what Jesus did with the young man—He bound him to the commandments of God. He wanted the man to admit he had fallen short of the divine standard. Jesus wanted him to understand he needed to get right with a holy God and not just have his psychological needs met.

B. The Ruler's Response (v. 20)

1. His perception of the law (v. 20*a*)

The response of the young man is incredible: "All these things have I kept from my youth up."

a) Externalizing the law

Maybe the rich young ruler never murdered anyone, committed adultery, stole anything, or lied. Perhaps he thought he honored his father and his mother. He probably did those things based on his external concept of righteous behavior. But when Jesus confronted him with an internal command such as loving his neighbor as himself, he was only deceiving himself when he said he kept them all. Now we know he's not telling the truth, so he violated the command of not bearing false witness. But the majority of Jews had so externalized the law that they never dealt with the heart.

b) Internalizing the law

In Matthew 5:21-37 Jesus internalizes the law with statements like these: "I know you don't think you murder, but when you hate someone, you commit murder in your heart. I know you don't think you commit adultery, but when you look on a woman with lust, you've committed adultery in your heart. When you divorce your wives without biblical grounds, you commit adultery as well. And I know you say you don't lie, but you lie through the phony oaths you make." Jesus confronts the people throughout Matthew 5. They might have looked good on the outside, but on the inside they were full of evil. The Ten Commandments are external behavior patterns that indicate right attitudes. It isn't enough to avoid killing someone; you also shouldn't hate the person. It isn't enough to avoid committing adultery; you shouldn't even desire it. The young man didn't understand the internal character of God's law; he only understood the external requirements. On the outside he believed he had kept all the commands.

What is amazing is that the man made his confession of righteousness in the presence of all the people. He must have believed that they would affirm his righteousness. And that was his problem. He had no sense of having violated God at all. Jesus couldn't take him on those terms—He had to open him up to his sin. Walter Chantry in his book *Today's Gospel: Authentic or Synthetic?* cites the following: "When you see that men have been wounded by the law, then it is time to pour in the balm of Gospel oil. It is the sharp needle of the law that makes way for the scarlet thread of the Gospel. You have to wound them before you can sew them up" ([Carlisle, Penn.: Banner of Truth, 1970], p. 43).

The young man didn't think he had a problem with sin. With that attitude he couldn't be saved. He didn't understand the meaning of salvation—that a sinner comes to God and asks for forgiveness. If you don't think you've sinned, you can't be saved.

21

The man diligently sought eternal life, so when he asked the right question, Jesus confronted him with his sin, but he wouldn't confess it. Confession of sin and repentance are essential in salvation. The Lord illustrates that for us here. The young man missed the point of God's law. He had externalized it, failing to understand that it was only a standard for measuring the heart.

2. His problem with self-righteousness (v. 20b)

At the end of Matthew 19:20 the young man says, "What lack I yet?" In his mind he had tried to keep the commandments and was convinced he did. That is the way self-righteous religion works. It is self-deceiving. The man believed he was righteous. He believed he had kept the law. That's why he couldn't figure out what he still needed to do. He had no idea he had fallen short of God's law.

Mark 10:21 says, "Then Jesus, beholding him, loved him." The man was sincere and genuine, and Jesus loved him. He is not willing that any should perish (2 Pet. 3:9). The Lord was about to die for the sins of that man, and He longed for the salvation of his soul. Nevertheless Jesus still wouldn't take him on his terms. The rich young ruler needed to understand his sinfulness.

There must be confession and repentance to obtain eternal life. They are a work of the Holy Spirit, not some pre-salvation human work. We are dependent on the Spirit of God for the realization that we have offended a holy God. Jesus wouldn't take the man unless he confessed his sin and understood that he must turn from it.

VII. SUBMIT TO THE LORD (vv. 21-22)

A. The Lord's Priority (v. 21)

Jesus went one step further for the man. In verse 21 He says, "If thou wilt be perfect, go and sell what thou hast, and give to the poor." The man claimed he loved his neighbor as himself, so Jesus told him to give everything he had to his neighbor as proof of his love. Jesus gave him a pre-salvation test. Jesus was saying in effect, "Are you going to do what I want you to do? Who runs your life? Do you or do I?" So He gave him a command. I believe true salvation includes submission to the Lord.

1. The priority of obedience

Now I don't believe a person who comes to Christ has a full understanding of all that submission to the lordship of Christ may mean. But I do believe the Lord wants him to be willing to confess and submit. Then Christ will unfold the fullness of what those things mean.

Jesus confronted the man's sin of covetousness. It was a sin of indulgence and materialism. He was indifferent to people who were poor and in need. So Jesus gave him the ultimate test: would he obey His lordship?

Do you have to give away everything you own to be a Christian? No. The Lord doesn't ask that. But you do have to be willing to do whatever the Lord asks of you. And what He asks depends on whom He's asking. In this case, the Lord isolated the main issue in the young man's life. We see the principle in Luke 14:33: "Whosoever he is of you that forsaketh not all that he hath, cannot be my disciple." So Jesus asked the man, "Are you willing to do what I tell you? I'm asking you to get rid of everything you own." He knew what was most important to the man. The most important thing for others might be a girl, a career, or a certain sin they want to indulge in. But for this man it was his money and possessions. And the Lord wanted him to be willing to give them up.

The willingness to give up what you have reminds me of the story of a slave and his master. The slave was a Christian; the master was not. The peace the slave had in his life was so evident that the master began to want it himself. One day he said to the slave, "How can I have what you have?" The slave said, "Put on your white suit, and come down here in the mud and work with us slaves." The master said, "I'll never do it. Why do I have to do that to be a Christian?" The slave said, "I'm just telling you that you have to do it." The master came back with the same

23

question several times and always received the same answer. Finally the master said, "I'm willing to do it because I want what you have." And the slave said, "Good. You don't have to do it. You just have to be willing to do it." In the same way, Jesus exposed the essence of the young ruler's heart. He was telling him, "Unless I become the number-one priority in your life, there will be no salvation for you."

2. The price of salvation

Salvation demands two things: acknowledging your offense to God and leaving your present priorities to follow Christ's commands, even if that should cost what is dearest to you. Salvation is a commitment to leave sin and follow Jesus Christ—at all costs. If you're not willing to be saved on those terms, Jesus won't take you.

The faith that will not save offers men some psychological relief from their anxiety but does not require a turning from sin and an affirmation of the lordship of Christ. In Matthew 13:44-46 are two parables—the parable of the hidden treasure and the parable of the pearl of great price. I believe both refer to the salvation that's offered in the kingdom. One man sold everything he had to buy the field to get the treasure; the other sold everything he had to buy the pearl. What they wanted cost everything they had. To come to Jesus Christ means to accept Him as the supreme Lord of your life. He becomes your first priority. I don't believe people understand the full implication of the lordship of Christ when they are first saved, but I do believe salvation involves a commitment. That's why Romans 10:9 says, "If thou shalt confess with thy mouth the *Lord* Jesus, and shalt believe in thine heart that God hath raised him from the dead, thou shalt be saved" (emphasis added). There's a price for salvation—it costs you all you possess.

B. The Ruler's Priority (v. 22)

The man was given a test because he was holding on to all he possessed. What was his reaction? Matthew 19:22 says, "But when the young man heard that saying, he went away sorrowful; for he had great possessions." Why did

24

he go away? Because his possessions were more important to him than Christ. He couldn't receive salvation on
those terms.

1. An honest reaction

Why does Matthew indicate that the man went away
sorrowful? Because there was some honesty in his
heart. He really did want eternal life; he just wasn't
willing to pay the price.

2. A happy reception

There is an example in Scripture of a man who had the
opposite reaction. Luke 19:1-6 says, "Jesus entered and
passed through Jericho. And, behold, there was a man,
named Zaccheus, who was the chief among the tax collectors; and he was rich. And he sought to see Jesus,
who he was, and could not because of the crowd; for he
was little of stature. And he ran ahead, and climbed up
into a sycamore tree to see him; for he was to pass that
way. And when Jesus came to the place, he looked up,
and saw him, and said unto him, Zaccheus, make
haste, and come down; for today I must abide at thy
house. And he made haste, and came down, and received Him joyfully." Why? Because he was a seeker,
too. Tax collectors don't usually lose their dignity by
climbing into trees to watch parades go by, but Zaccheus did because he was a true seeker.

Verses 7-8 record what happened as a result of Christ's
visit: "When they saw it, they all murmured, saying
that he was gone to be guest with a man that is a sinner. And Zaccheus stood, and said unto the Lord, Behold, Lord, the half of my goods I give to the poor; and
if I have taken anything from any man by false accusation, I restore him fourfold." He knew he had been doing wrong all the time and that he needed to get his life
right. He realized he had to return four hundred per-
cent on all he had extorted from the poor. That certainly is opposite the attitude of the young ruler. Jesus
said, "This day is salvation come to this house, forso-
much as he also is a son of Abraham" (v. 9). Zaccheus
became a true Jew. Why did salvation come to him? Be-

cause he could think only of what a sinner he was. He wanted to give back all the things he took unjustly, plus half of all he had. Therefore Jesus said, "The Son of man is come to seek and to save that which was lost" (v. 10).

The story of the young man in Matthew 19 is a sad one. He wasn't willing to make the commitment that Zaccheus did. The Lord showed him he was a sinner by measuring him against the law of God, but he refused to see his sin. The Lord gave him a command and asked him to follow, but he wouldn't do either. He could not receive salvation because he wasn't willing to turn from his sin and affirm the lordship of Jesus Christ in his life. I repeat what Matthew says in 19:22, "He went away sorrowful; for he had great possessions." He came for eternal life and left without it.

Focusing on the Facts

1. What truth is presented in Luke 14:33 (see p. 8)?
2. Why did the young man in Matthew 19:16-22 go away without receiving eternal life (see pp. 9-10)?
3. What is wrong with much contemporary evangelism (see p. 10)?
4. Why was the young ruler seeking eternal life (see p. 10)?
5. Describe some of the characteristics of the young ruler (see p. 11).
6. Define eternal life (see p. 11).
7. How do we know that the young ruler diligently sought eternal life (Mark 10:17; see p. 12)?
8. Why was the young ruler's motive incomplete (see p. 13)?
9. In what way did the young ruler acknowledge Jesus as "good" (see p. 14)?
10. In Matthew 19:16 the ruler asks Jesus, "What good thing shall I do?" Explain why that was a fair question to ask (see p. 15).
11. What did Jesus remind the young man that he needed to do to enter into eternal life (Matt. 19:17; see p. 16)?
12. What did Jesus have to confront the young man about (see p. 17)?
13. When you share the gospel with others, what should you make sure they understand (see p. 18)?

14. No one can understand what _____ means unless he understands what _____ _____ requires (see p. 20)?
15. Explain the young man's perception of keeping God's law (see p. 20)?
16. How did Jesus define what keeping God's law means (Matt. 5:21-37; see pp. 20-21)?
17. What is characteristic of self-righteousness religions (see p. 22)?
18. The young ruler claimed that he loved his neighbor as himself. What did Jesus ask him to do that proved he didn't (Matt. 19:21; see pp. 22-23)?
19. What sin of the ruler's did Jesus confront? What did Jesus want him to do (see p. 23)?
20. What kind of faith will not save a man (see p. 24)?
21. Explain how Zaccheus's response to Jesus was different from that of the young ruler (Luke 19:1-10; see pp. 25-26).

Pondering the Principles

1. Look up the following verses: John 10:27-28; 17:3; Romans 6:23; Hebrews 5:8-9; and 1 John 5:11-13, 20. What does each say about how we obtain eternal life? Which verses indicate that possessing eternal life is related to knowing Jesus Christ? What are the benefits of possessing eternal life? How does one know for sure that he has eternal life?

2. Read Matthew 5-7. As you read, record what you believe to be your level of growth in regard to each area of godly living that Christ names. Be honest in your evaluation. After your evaluation is complete, you ought to be ready to kneel before God and thank Him for the grace He has bestowed on you through Christ. Take time to draw near to God as you confess your sinfulness. Be humble in your approach and allow God to exalt you (James 4:8, 10).

3. Based on this study, what changes do you need to make in your presentation of the gospel? What aspects of your presentation were affirmed by this lesson? As you evangelize the lost, remember to emphasize the reasons they are lost and their need to confess Christ as Lord.

2
The Poverty of Riches—The Riches of Poverty

Outline

Introduction

Lesson
I. The Poverty of Riches (vv. 23-26)
   A. The Restriction for the Rich (vv. 23-24)
      1. The decree of difficulty (v. 23)
      2. The degree of difficulty (v. 24)
         a) The phrase interpreted
            (1) The proper interpretation
            (2) The improper interpretations
               (*a*) A needle gate
               (*b*) A scribal error
               (*c*) A molecular change
         b) The principles identified
            (1) Rich people have false security
            (2) Rich people are bound to this world
               (*a*) The contentment of the godly
               (*b*) The captivity of the rich
                  i) Choked by riches
                  ii) Captured by folly
            (3) Rich people are selfish
   B. The Reaction of the Disciples (v. 25)
      1. Their exclamation (v. 25*a*)
      2. Their question (v. 25*b*)
   C. The Resource of Salvation (v. 26)
      1. It's impossible with men (v. 26*a*)
      2. It's possible with God (v. 26*b*)

II. The Riches of Poverty (vv. 27-29)
  A. The Faithfulness of the Disciples (v. 27)
    1. The affirmation (v. 27*a*)
    2. The anticipation (v. 27*b*)
  B. The Future for True Believers (vv. 28-29)
    1. Sharing in the triumph of Christ (v. 28)
      a) The rebirth of the earth
      b) The reign of Christ
    2. Receiving more than they gave up (v. 29*a*)
      a) The price of salvation
      b) The reward of salvation
    3. Inheriting eternal life (v. 29*b*)

Introduction

Matthew 19:23-29 follows the Lord's encounter with the rich young ruler who refused eternal life because he wouldn't accept the Lord's terms. Out of that experience comes the Lord's teaching about true riches and true poverty. Proverbs 13:7 sums up the lesson of our text: "There is he that maketh himself rich, yet hath nothing; there is he that maketh himself poor, yet hath great riches." That is a paradoxical truth. The Bible has a lot to say about both riches and poverty. Yet there is perhaps no more direct passage than what is taught in Matthew 19:23-29 by our Lord.

Lesson

I. THE POVERTY OF RICHES (vv. 23-26)

  A. The Restriction for the Rich (vv. 23-24)

    1. The decree of difficulty (v. 23)

      "Then said Jesus unto his disciples, Verily I say unto you that a rich man shall with difficulty enter into the kingdom of heaven."

      The term "kingdom of heaven" is synonymous with the term "kingdom of God" (v. 24). They both refer to the sphere of God's gracious rule. They are both synonyms for eternal life and salvation. In Matthew 19:16 the young man says, "What good thing shall I do, that I may have eternal life?" In verse 23 Jesus refers to eternal life as entering "into the kingdom of heaven."

Our Lord is making a clear statement: it's extremely difficult for rich people to be saved. The young man was not willing to forsake all and follow the Lord. Jesus had reiterated the importance of being willing many times. In Matthew 10:38 He says, "He that taketh not his cross and followeth after me, is not worthy of me" (cf. Matt. 16:24). In Mark 10:21 Jesus says to the rich young ruler, "Sell whatever thou hast . . . take up the cross, and follow me." To take up one's cross is to be willing to die. You've got to be willing to abandon everything, even your own life, if Jesus requires it. A person must strip himself to go through the narrow gate that leads to salvation (Matt. 7:13-14). The young man was not willing to admit his sinfulness or to say no to all that he possessed. The price of salvation was too high for him.

Jesus draws this conclusion: "Verily, I say unto you that a rich man shall with difficulty [Gk., *duskolōs*] enter into the kingdom of God" (v. 23). That Greek word is only used three times in the New Testament, and each time in a gospel account of this passage (cf. Mark 10:23; Luke 18:24). It is difficult for a rich man to enter salvation, but how difficult is it? The answer comes in the next verse.

2. The degree of difficulty (v. 24)

"Again I say unto you, It is easier for a camel to go through the eye of a needle, than for a rich man to enter into the kingdom of God."

a) The phrase interpreted

How difficult is it to stick a camel through the eye of a needle? It's impossible! You can't put a camel through the eye of a needle.

(1) The proper interpretation

31

Where did that phrase come from? It was a colloquial expression. The Talmud alludes to the Babylonian saying of putting an elephant through the eye of a needle (*Temurah* 21a). It was used to express something that was impossible. Since there were no elephants in Palestine, the Lord simply substituted a camel for an elephant to make the phrase relevant. So how difficult is it for rich people to get saved? It's impossible.

(2) The improper interpretations

It is important to understand that the phrase means just what it says: salvation for a rich man is just as impossible as sticking a camel through the eye of a needle. Yet it is amazing what people will do to avoid that interpretation. They want to make it difficult but not impossible.

(*a*) A needle gate

Some claim that the needle refers to a gate in one of the walls of Jerusalem. It was supposedly so small that when anyone wanted to take his camel through it, he had to unload everything off the camel's back, make him kneel down on all fours, and force him through the needle gate. There are several problems with that view. First, verse 24 doesn't say "needle gate"; it says "needle." Second, we know that the phrase was a colloquialism that was extant at the time our Lord used it. And finally, we have no proof that there ever was such a gate in Jerusalem! Even if there were, the people weren't stupid: they wouldn't jam their camels through a tiny gate when a huge gate was only fifty feet further up the road.

(*b*) A scribal error

The Greek word for "camel" is *kamēlos* while the Greek word for the cable that was used to tie up a ship is *kamilos*—a difference of one vowel. Some say that a scribal error caused *cable* to become *camel*. But that interpretation doesn't help because you can't stick a cable through a needle either. Also, it's not reasonable to that every scribe would make that mistake. And if we started to explain the Bible on the basis of possible scribal errors, we could make any passage say whatever we wanted it to say.

(c) A molecular change

Some have suggested that if you could line up the molecules in a camel, you could shoot him through the eye of a needle. One individual even suggested that if you reduced a camel to liquid, you could put him through the eye of a needle with an eyedropper! But there is no need for such extreme interpretations.

b) The principles identified

It is not difficult to enter the kingdom; it is impossible. That's what our Lord has in mind in Matthew 7:14 when He says, "Narrow is the gate, and hard is the way, which leadeth into life, and few there be that find it." In Matthew 11:12 He says, "The violent take [the kingdom] by force." They fight to get in.

It is impossible to be saved when you come for salvation on human terms. Jesus is saying, "I demand the impossible." No one can get saved on his own terms. In one fell swoop Jesus eliminates all works-righteousness systems. Many Christians say, "Salvation is easy. Just believe." The young ruler was ready to do that, but the Lord put up impassable barriers. When the man refused to accept Jesus' terms, salvation became impossible for him. He had no power to do it himself. Jeremiah 13:23 says, "Can the Ethiopian change his skin, or the leopard his spots? Then may ye also do good, that are accustomed to do evil." Man can't be saved by himself.

33

No amount of works, religion, activity, desire, or willfulness will work—it's impossible.

The impossibility of salvation is crystallized in the case of rich people for three reasons.

(1) Rich people have false security

The rich can't save themselves because they believe they don't need God. They have all the resources they think they will ever need. There is no need for them to depend on God.

The city of Laodicea was one of the wealthiest of all the cities in Asia Minor. In A.D. 60 it was flattened by an earthquake. The Roman government commissioned several emissaries to go to Laodicea to help finance the rebuilding of the city. But the rulers of Laodicea refused their help. The people of Laodicea raised their entire city out of the ashes without taking a dime from the Roman government, which swelled their pride. That attitude spilled over to the church, which became the dead Laodicean church (Rev. 3:14-19). The Lord told them, "Thou sayest, I am rich, and increased with goods, and have need of nothing, and knowest not that thou art wretched, and miserable, and poor, and blind, and naked" (v. 17).

Instructions for the Rich

Rich people tend to feel smugly complacent. Paul wrote to Timothy under the inspiration of the Holy Spirit about how to minister to the rich (1 Tim. 6:17-19).

1. Trust in God

He said, "Charge them that are rich in this age, that they be not high-minded, nor trust in uncertain riches but in the living God, who giveth us richly all things to enjoy" (v. 17). It is the particular problem of rich people to trust in their uncertain riches and believe they don't need God—they think they can buy anything they need.

2. Give to the needy

The apostle Paul said rich people are to be told to "do good, that they be rich in good works, ready to distribute, willing to share" (v. 18). Why should a rich man be told those things? Because if he's not willing to submit everything to the lordship of Christ, the gospel is meaningless to him. When you present the gospel to a rich man, don't say, "Wouldn't you like to ask Jesus in your heart? We'll worry about all the other stuff later." That isn't a biblical approach. If a rich man comes to you, the best question you can ask him is: "If the Lord Jesus wants every dime you have, will you give it to Him?" If he isn't willing, you can end the discussion there.

3. Obtain eternal life

If rich people will do good and be ready to share what they have with others, they'll lay "up in store for themselves a good foundation against the time to come, that they may lay hold on eternal life" (v. 19). The Greek word used in verse 19 is not *aiōnios*, which means "eternal life" but *ontōs*, which means "real life." Life does not consist in the abundance of the things a man possesses (Luke 12:15). But the rich believe real life is in money.

The rich man doesn't get saved by giving away his money, but doing so demonstrates that he is more concerned with the lordship of Christ than with holding onto his resources. When anyone comes to Christ, he must come on Christ's terms: forsaking all and following Him. That doesn't mean He'll take away all you have. He may give you more than you can handle, like He did for Abraham. Or, like Job, He may give you back far more than He ever took from you. But the issue is not whether He will or won't but whether you're willing to let Him do it.

(2) Rich people are bound to this world

(a) The contentment of the godly

First Timothy 6:6 says, "Godliness with contentment is great gain." Have you ever met a totally contented person? Most people in our materialistic society aren't content because they want something they don't have. Paul continued, "We brought nothing into this world, and it is certain we can carry nothing out. And having food and raiment let us be therewith content" (vv. 7-8).

(b) The captivity of the rich

Paul said, "They that will be rich fall into temptation and a snare, and into many foolish and hurtful lusts, which drown men in destruction and perdition. For the love of money is the root of all evil, which, while some coveted after, they have erred from the faith, and pierced themselves through with many sorrows" (vv. 9-10). For rich people, everything revolves around this world: how much they have in the bank, how many possessions they have, or how many cars they have. Jesus said, "Where your treasure is, there will your heart be also" (Matt. 6:21). If all a man cares about is in this world, then he has no thought for the heavenly realm. When he is confronted with the gospel and learns that Christ wants him to subject all his money and possessions to His lordship, he won't give them up.

i) Choked by riches

Jesus said that the seed on the thorny ground represented "the cares of this age, and the deceitfulness of riches, and the lusts of other things entering in, choke the word, and it becometh unfruitful" (Mark 4:19). There are people who hear the gospel and say, "Oh, isn't that wonderful?" They respond, but soon they are deceived by their substantial riches, and they abandon the gospel.

36

The concerns people have for things in this world need to be dealt with first before the gospel will ever be fruitful in their lives. It is impossible for rich people to be saved because they are bound to this world in their humanness. They live and die for their possessions and trust in them as their security.

ii) Captured by folly

Luke 12:16-21 is a parable about a big fool: "The ground of a certain rich man brought forth plentifully. And he thought within himself, saying, What shall I do, because I have no place to bestow my crops? And he said, This will I do: I will pull down my barns, and build greater; and there will I bestow all my crops and my goods. And I will say to my soul, Soul, thou hast much goods laid up for many years; take thine ease. Eat, drink, and be merry. But God said unto him, Thou fool, this night thy soul shall be required of thee; then whose shall those things be, which thou hast provided? So is he that layeth up treasure for himself, and is not rich toward God."

Don't stockpile for some unknown future. You are a steward of whatever God has given you. Use it for the advance of His kingdom and the glory of His name. Lay up eternal treasure right now.

Rich people are bound to the world because their only hope is in their money.

(3) Rich people are selfish

I know a man who works for a multi-millionaire whose holdings total about $300 million. He said all the millionaires he has worked for have three things in common: they are capable of being richer, they are eccentric, and they are extremely self-centered. The rich indulge themselves.

Luke 16:19-31 is the story about a rich man and a beggar named Lazarus. The rich man fared sumptuously every day while Lazarus laid in the gutter begging for crumbs from the rich man's table. The dogs were even licking his sores as he lay in the gutter. What kind of a man would sit by and allow that to happen? The rich man ended up in hell while the beggar was in Abraham's bosom being comforted.

The world is full of people who indulge themselves. It's impossible for rich people to be saved because they can't overcome their humanness. And their evil nature manifests itself in the love of money and possessions.

Rabbinical Teaching on Riches

Jesus shocked the rich young ruler, and also the disciples, when He said it was impossible for the rich to be saved. The rich young ruler had been taught differently. He no doubt had been instructed from rabbinical Judaism, and perhaps was even the ruler of a synagogue. The rabbis taught that one should never give away more than one fifth of what he possessed. Doing so was thought to be unlawful and sinful. That law allowed them to appear holy yet be selfish. If they could continue to pile up riches and call it the blessing of God, and then give away one little part of it, they thought they could buy their way into the kingdom. They believed that the larger the fifth they gave away, the more they were assured of purchasing salvation.

Note the following quotations from the Apocrypha: Tobit 12:8 says, "It is better to give alms than to store up gold; for almsgiving saves one from death and expiates every sin." Sirach 3:29 says, "Alms atone for sins." The Talmud says that alms-giving is more excellent than all offerings and is equal to the whole law and will deliver from the condemnation of hell and make one perfectly righteous (cf. *Baba Bathra 10a*). So, the more money one had, the more he could give; and the more he could give, the more he seemed assured of purchasing his salvation, and the higher his status became in the kingdom. But Jesus says that the richer you are, the harder salvation becomes. That was a shocking statement to those who thought they could buy their way into the kingdom.

B. The Reaction of the Disciples (v. 25)

1. Their exclamation (v. 25a)

"When his disciples heard it, they were exceedingly amazed."

That means they were dumbfounded, thinking, *Is He saying rich people can't enter the kingdom?* Christ's teaching was contrary to everything they had been taught from tradition. The disciples thought rich people could atone for everything. They could fill the thirteen trumpet-shaped receptacles that lined the court of the women in the Temple. But Jesus was saying that it is impossible to enter the kingdom by giving alms. No wonder James said, "Come now, ye rich men, weep and howl for your miseries that shall come upon you" (James 5:1).

2. Their question (v. 25b)

"Who, then, can be saved?"

If rich people can't be saved, who can be? Poor people couldn't even purchase significant sacrifices. If it is impossible for rich people to be saved, it certainly would be impossible for everyone else.

C. The Resource of Salvation (v. 26)

1. It's impossible with men (v. 26a)

"Jesus beheld them, and said unto them, With men this is impossible."

Salvation is impossible on human terms. You can't overcome your own sinful nature. Rich people can't overcome their dependency on riches, their love of things in this world, and the consumptive selfishness that characterizes their life-style. Salvation is impossible for men. With one statement Jesus wiped out all works-righteousness systems. All the religions in the world can't save men. It's not just difficult; it's impossible.

2. It's possible with God (v. 26b)

"But with God all things are possible."

Even rich people can be saved. Humanly speaking, they are tougher to save than others, but with God all things are possible. That's good news. Why is God the only one who can save men? Because only God can change the heart.

The rich young ruler came to Christ to be saved, which was asking for something that was impossible. When he went away unsaved, that confirmed the impossibility of salvation. The young ruler demonstrated that salvation is impossible on human terms. Repentance and the affirmation of the lordship of Jesus Christ is mandatory for salvation. That is not being taught today, but it needs to be. Only God can overcome the love of money, selfishness, and an earth-bound mentality. Only God can change man's heart. John 1:12-13 says, "As many as received him, to them gave he power to become the children of God, even to them that believed on his name; who were born not of blood, nor of the will of the flesh, nor of the will of man, but of God." Only God can save a man.

Gentle Evangelism

Second Timothy 2:24 says that the servant of the Lord doesn't fight. When we present the truth of Jesus Christ, we should "be gentle unto all men, apt to teach, patient, in meekness instructing those that oppose him" (vv. 24-25). We are not to intimidate or badger people to repent. We are to teach them gently and patiently, recognizing that only God can "give them repentance to the acknowledging of the truth" (v. 25). We don't know if God will give them repentance, for it's something only God can do. In John

6:65 Jesus says, "No man can come unto me, except it were given unto him of my Father." Evangelists must be gentle, patient, and meek to those who oppose the gospel. Yet they must be careful not to manipulate people. We can only beseech God that He would grant repentance.

Am I Preaching Salvation by Works?

Some people have accused me of preaching salvation by works because I feel so strongly about repentance. To those people I would answer with 2 Timothy 2:25-26: God must give the unsaved "repentance to the acknowledging of the truth . . . that they may recover themselves out of the snare of the devil." Repentance is an element of salvation that only God can perform. There is no work involved here. I'm not attempting to say that repentance or an affirmation of the lordship of Christ is a pre-salvation, human work. But I am saying that where real salvation occurs, God brings about repentance, submission, and a forsaking of everything to follow Christ. That is no less the work of God than the redemptive transaction itself.

II. THE RICHES OF POVERTY (vv. 27-29)

A. The Faithfulness of the Disciples (v. 27)

1. The affirmation (v. 27a)

"Then answered Peter and said unto him, Behold, we have forsaken all, and followed thee."

Peter is affirming that the disciples came to Christ on His terms. The rich young ruler didn't, and they could see the contrast. He went away sorrowing, unwilling to forsake all and follow Christ. The disciples left their nets and their tax tables. They said good-bye to their employment and their families. They left everything to follow Him. They took up their crosses and denied themselves. Peter's statement in verse 27 was his definition of salvation. He hadn't seen the crucifixion or the resurrection yet, so on this side of the cross he saw salvation as the Lord presented it—a forsaking of sin and

41

a following after Christ. Salvation is submitting to Christ's direction and lordship.

There was one disciple who was not a legitimate follower, but Peter didn't know that at the time. Judas never abandoned his love of money. When he knew he wasn't going to receive the money he thought would come his way through his involvement in this new political entity called the kingdom, he tried to receive as much as he could by selling out the Savior. His intention was to grab the money and run. But the guilt was overwhelming, and he killed himself. It was only on the outside that Judas appeared as if he had forsaken all and followed Christ.

2. The anticipation (v. 27*b*)

"What shall we have, therefore?"

The rich man kept all his riches but lost eternal life. The disciples had abandoned everything in life, and they wanted to know what they would gain. That's not a bad question to ask. After all, they had followed Christ in anticipation of the kingdom. They followed Him hoping that He would right the nation of Israel and throw off the Roman yoke. They hoped He would bring in the glorious splendor the prophets had spoken of. I think Peter's heart was right as he summed up all the anxiety of the disciples by asking, "What's in it for us? What are we going to receive?" I don't believe Peter was totally frustrated—just partially. He was interested in what Christ had to say about what God had prepared for them. Since they came to Christ on His terms, they wanted to know the benefits of their salvation.

B. The Future for True Believers (vv. 28-29)

1. Sharing in the triumph of Christ (v. 28)

"And Jesus said to them, Verily I say unto you that ye who have followed me, in the regeneration, when the Son of man shall sit on the throne of his glory, ye shall also sit upon twelve thrones, judging the twelve tribes of Israel."

42

a) The rebirth of the earth

What is "the regeneration"? The Greek word for "regeneration" is *palingenesia*, and it refers to the millennial kingdom. It is used in only one other place in the New Testament and that's in Titus 3:5. There the word refers to our new birth in Christ. In Matthew 19:28 Jesus is talking about the rebirth of the earth. That rebirth is a perfect parallel to our individual *palingenesia* as we are born again in Christ. Just as our new birth is incomplete until we enter heaven, the earth awaits its rebirth in the millennial kingdom. We wait for the new heaven, and the earth waits for the new earth.

b) The reign of Christ

In Matthew 19:28 our Lord is talking about the millennial kingdom, when He will sit on the throne of His glory. Psalm 2:9 indicates that the Lord Jesus Christ is going to rule the nations with a rod of iron. He is going to be the King of kings and Lord of lords (Rev. 19:16). He's coming to reign in glory and power. He's coming to rule the earth for a thousand years, and the saints will reign with Him (Rev. 20:4-6). The Old Testament saints (Dan. 7:18), New Testament saints (1 Cor. 6:2), Tribulation saints (Rev. 20:4), and the apostles (Matt. 19:28) will all be there. All the redeemed of all ages will reign with Christ when He sits on the throne of His glory. He will come in power and glory after the Tribulation (Matt. 24:29-30). He will then set up His kingdom of glory and rule for a thousand years. At that time the nation of Israel will be restored and the twelve apostles—with Matthias supplanting Judas (Acts 1:15-26) —will guide and judge the tribes of Israel.

In Acts 3:21 Peter calls the millennial kingdom the "times of restitution" when the earth rests from the curse and is restored to its original state before the Fall. Matthew 12:32 calls it the age to come. According to the prophets, it is the time when truth will dominate, righteousness will flourish, peace will prevail, and joy will abound on the earth. It is the time when the Holy Spirit's power will be demonstrated, and Satan will be bound. Jerusalem will be exalted. Life will be long because health and healing will be prevalent. The earth will produce food like never before. The desert will blossom like a rose. It is in this great millennial kingdom that the twelve disciples will sit on the twelve thrones—places of rulership over the twelve tribes of Israel.

The first thing that comes to the poor of this world is that they will share in the triumph of Christ. We are going to rule with Christ. First Peter 2:9 calls us a royal priesthood.

2. Receiving more than they gave up (v. 29*a*)

"Every one that hath forsaken houses, or brethren, or sisters, or father, or mother, or wife, or children, or lands, for my name's sake, shall receive an hundredfold."

a) The price of salvation

Christ is acknowledging that when you came to Him, you might have had to turn your back on a relationship. Becoming a Christian may alienate you from your spouse. It probably won't cause a divorce, but there may be a recognizable division. Perhaps you were alienated from your parents or your brothers and sisters. Maybe you were kicked out of your family when you came to Christ and lost an inheritance. There may have been a price to pay, but no one has forsaken anything for Christ's sake that he won't receive back a hundredfold. When you gave up your family, you inherited all those in the Body of Christ: you have mothers, fathers, brothers, sisters, uncles, aunts, husbands, wives, houses, and lands worldwide. You are embraced by a fellowship of those who love the Lord Jesus Christ.

b) The reward of salvation

The hundredfold you receive isn't just future. Mark 10:30 gives the same list as Matthew 19:29 but precedes it with, "Now in this time." When you meet a Christian for the first time, isn't it amazing how immediate the bond becomes? You may travel somewhere and find a home to stay in and someone to provide a meal for you. You meet a family of people who love Christ. There's far more compensation in the family of God than anything you ever give up. Whenever you think about what you gave up, just look at what you have gained.

3. Inheriting eternal life (v. 29*b*)

"And shall inherit everlasting life."

The poor will be rewarded for eternity. I think what Christ means is that they will enter into the fullness of what God has planned in eternity. We'll be blessed now and in the kingdom. Ultimately we will have the fullness of all that God has prepared for us in eternity. We will receive our full inheritance—the completion of salvation for which our bodies now groan, awaiting their redemption (Rom. 8:23). First Corinthians 15:53 says, "This corruptible must put on incorruption, and this mortal must put on immortality." It is then that this marvelous thing will come to pass: "We shall be like [Christ]; for we shall see him as he is" (1 John 3:2). Ephesians 2:7 says, "In the ages to come he [will] show the exceeding riches of his grace in his kindness toward us through Christ Jesus."

To be poor in this life for the sake of Christ is to be rich here and now with houses, lands, and relationships. And then we will be rich in the kingdom, reigning with Christ. Take your choice: rich now, poor forever; or poor now, rich forever. If you're willing to be poor, God may make you rich, even in this life. But keep this in mind. I'm poor in the sense that I don't own any of what I do have. The Lord keeps depositing it with me to see how I manage it. That's a helpful perspective. None of the things I have are mine; they're all His. I gave up everything when I came to Christ. But He has a lot that He sorts out among us to manage for His glory in advance of His kingdom. Jim Elliot, a missionary who was murdered by the Auca Indians in Ecuador some years ago, said, "He is no fool who gives up what he cannot keep to gain what he cannot lose."

Focusing on the Facts

1. Are the terms "kingdom of heaven" and "kingdom of God" synonymous? To what do they refer (see p. 30)?
2. What did Jesus mean by telling men to take up their crosses (see p. 31)?
3. Where did the phrase "it is easier for a camel to go through the eye of a needle" come from? What does it tell us about rich people getting to heaven (see p. 32)?
4. What are some of the erroneous interpretations of that phrase? What are the people who come up with those interpretations trying to make Matthew 19:24 say (see pp. 32-33)?
5. Why is salvation impossible for men on their own terms (see p. 33)?
6. Why is it impossible for the rich to be saved (see pp. 34-37)?
7. What were the instructions that Paul gave Timothy regarding his ministry to the rich (1 Tim. 6:17-19; see pp. 34-35)?
8. Why are many people in our society discontent (see p. 36)?
9. What must rich people deal with first in their lives before the gospel will ever become fruitful (see pp. 36-37)?
10. Relate some of the teaching that Jewish leaders, such as the rich young ruler, received from the rabbinical schools (see p. 38).
11. Why were the disciples "exceedingly amazed" after hearing Jesus speak about the impossibility of salvation for the rich (Matt. 19:25; see p. 39)?
12. How is it possible for all men to be saved? Why is that the only way men can be saved (Matt. 19:26; see pp. 39-40)?
13. When we present the gospel to the unsaved, what kind of attitude should we adopt? Why (2 Tim. 2:24-25; see p. 40)?
14. Explain why the need for repentance and a submission to the lordship of Christ are not pre-salvation, human works (see p. 41)?
15. What did Peter affirm in Matthew 19:27? Which disciple was he mistaken about (see pp. 41-42)?
16. What were the benefits that the disciples would receive for forsaking all and following Christ (Matt. 19:28-29; see pp. 42-45)?
17. What does the word *regeneration* refer to in Matthew 19:28 (see p. 43)?

18. Who will reign with Christ when He sits on His throne of glory (see p. 43)?
19. What does Christ promise to give in return for what we forsake to come to Him (Matt. 19:29; see p. 44)?

Pondering the Principles

1. Review the reasons for the impossibility of salvation for the rich (see pp. 34-38). Examine your life in light of those reasons. Is there a sense in which you gain a certain amount of security in your resources and possessions? In what ways do you see that your dependence on those things binds you to this world? Be specific. To what degree do you see a selfish attitude in your life? Can it be traced to your dependence on your money and possessions, and if so, how? As a Christian who has been given salvation because of God's grace, you should be totally dependent on God and not on your money and possessions. How can you specifically apply Paul's instructions to Timothy regarding the rich (see 1 Tim. 6:17-19)?

2. Review the section on the benefits of salvation for true believers (see pp. 42-45). Two of those benefits are future, and one is both present and future. Thank God for the future you will spend with Christ in eternity. Many of you can thank Him for one of the benefits of salvation right now. Make a list of what God has given you that you could classify as being more than what you gave up. Offer God praise for each one.

3

Equality in the Kingdom

Outline

Introduction
A. God Treats People Equally
   1. The defense of Ezekiel
   2. The defense of the New Testament
     a) Romans 2:9-11
     b) Colossians 3:24-25
B. God Gives Salvation Equally

Lesson
  I. The Proverb
   A. The Riddle Defined
   B. The Riddle Solved
 II. The Parable
   A. The Scene Set (v. 1)
     1. The owner introduced
     2. The work illuminated
       a) The time of day
       b) The type of work
       c) The time of harvest
     3. The laborers identified
       a) Their classification
       b) Their wage
   B. The Laborers Hired (vv. 2-7)
     1. The first group (v. 2)
     2. The second group (vv. 3-4)
     3. The third and fourth groups (v. 5)
     4. The last group (vv. 6-7)
   C. The Laborers Rewarded (vv. 8-15)
     1. The generosity of the owner (vv. 8-9)
     2. The grumblings of the last in line (vv. 10-12)

Introduction

A. God Treats People Equally

  1. The defense of Ezekiel

One of the great men of God in the Old Testament was the prophet Ezekiel. Prophets like Ezekiel were common in the land of Israel. One of the duties of those spokesmen for God was to warn the people about sin. Ezekiel often reminded the children of Israel of the sins that had caused them to be taken into Babylonian captivity so they wouldn't repeat them. One of the things that had caused God's judgment upon them was their accusing God of being unfair. That attack was leveled against God's nature and character. Ezekiel 18:25 says, "Ye say, The way of the Lord is not equal. Here now, O house of Israel, is not my way equal? Are not your ways unequal?" The same thing is repeated in verse 29. God is a God of perfect equality. If we believe He isn't, then it's our ways that are unequal. God is the standard, not us.

2. The defense of the New Testament

That wasn't the first or last time God has been accused of being unfair. The writers of Scripture took on that accusation repeatedly. At least a half-dozen times this statement is made in the New Testament: "God is no respecter of persons." That's another way of saying God treats everyone equally.

a) Romans 2:9-11—The apostle Paul said, "Tribulation and anguish, upon every soul of man that doeth evil, of the Jew first, and also of the Greek; but glory, honor, and peace, to every man that worketh good, to the Jew first, and also to the Greek; for there is no respect of persons with God." Those who don't know God will be judged, and those who do know God will be blessed.

b) Colossians 3:24-25—"Knowing that of the Lord, ye shall receive the reward of the inheritance; for ye serve the Lord Christ. But he that doeth wrong shall receive for the wrong which he hath done, and there is no respect of persons."

God rewards those who do right and judges those who do wrong. He has no regard for their individual personalities.

B. God Gives Salvation Equally

God also gives the blessings of salvation equally to all. All who come to the Lord Jesus Christ receive the same salvation—no one receives any more or any less. No matter what the circumstances are and no matter how diligent or faithful our service, it is God's pleasure to give us the same salvation.

Let's look at Matthew 19:30—20:16: "Many that are first shall be last, and the last shall be first. For the kingdom of heaven is like a man that is an householder, who went out early in the morning to hire laborers into his vineyard. And when he had agreed with the laborers for a denarius a day, he sent them into his vineyard. And he went out about the third hour, and saw others standing idle in the market place, and said unto them, Go ye also into the vineyard, and whatever is right, I will give you. And they went their way. Again he went out about the sixth and ninth hour, and did the same. And about the eleventh hour he went out, and found others standing idle, and saith unto them, Why stand ye here all the day idle? They say unto him, Because no man hath hired us. He saith unto them, Go ye also into the vineyard, and whatever is right, that shall ye receive. So when evening was come, the lord of the vineyard saith unto his steward, Call the laborers, and give them their hire, beginning from the last unto the first. And when they came that were hired about the eleventh hour, they received every man a denarius. But when the first came, they supposed that they should have received more; and they likewise received every man a denarius. And when they had received it, they murmured against the householder, saying, These last have worked but one hour, and thou hast made them equal unto us, who have borne the burden and heat of the day. But he answered one of them, and said, Friend, I do thee no wrong. Didst not thou agree with me for a denarius? Take what is thine, and go thy way; I will give unto this last, even as unto thee. Is it not lawful for me to do what I will with mine own? Is thine eye evil, because I am good? So the last shall be first, and the first last."

Notice that the parable is bracketed by a repetition of the same proverb: "Many that are first shall be last, and the last shall be first. . . . The last shall be first, and the first last." It is apparent that the parable is designed to illustrate that maxim. To understand what our Lord is teaching we will look at four elements: the proverb, the parable, the point, and the principles.

Lesson

I. THE PROVERB

    A. The Riddle Defined

        A proverb is a short statement of wisdom, usually of unknown or ancient origin. In this case it is this: the first shall be last, and the last shall be first. Now it may be that the Lord borrowed this particular proverb from His own day. We don't have any evidence of it in any other writings, but it may have been a common statement. Perhaps He coined it Himself. We do know He used it on several occasions. So it was certainly a part of His teaching.

B. The Riddle Solved

Some proverbs come in the form of a riddle, and this is one of them. It's hard to know what it means when you first read it. What do "first" and "last" refer to? Before I began to study this passage, I mulled over the parable in my mind. The one thing that stood out was that everyone would be the same. In a typical race, someone finishes first, someone finishes last, and some finish in the middle. But in this race everyone crosses the finish line at the same time. In a sense, the last are first, and the first are last. All are the same.

II. THE PARABLE

A. The Scene Set (v. 1)

Matthew 20:1 says, "The kingdom of heaven is like a man that is an householder, who went out early in the morning to hire laborers into his vineyard." Christ is discussing the kingdom of heaven, which means this is a spiritual lesson. We're not talking about earthly things; we're talking about things in the sphere of God's domain. For us to understand the spiritual dimension, we need an earthly illustration because we're earthly-minded. Parables are earthly illustrations.

1. The owner introduced

Jesus begins the parable by introducing us to a man who is what the Greek text labels an *oikodespotēs*—*oikos* means "house" and *despotēs* means "ruler." Verse 15 says, "Is it not lawful for me to do what I will with mine own?" The money he paid the laborers was his own, which indicates that he was the owner.

2. The work illuminated

a) The time of day

Incorporated within the man's estate was a vineyard. Verse 1 says he went out early in the morning. That means he went out prior to 6:00 A.M. The Jewish day began at six in the morning and ended at six at night. They worked a twelve-hour day. So he went into town to hire laborers to work in his vineyard.

b) The type of work

The Jews were familiar with vineyards. The land of Palestine is divided into two basic types of land: plains and mountain slopes. The plains, such as the valley of the Jordan, the valley of Sharon, and the valley of Esdraelon (otherwise known as the plain of Megiddo where Armageddon will be centered), are characterized by grain fields. The slopes of the mountains are terraced for the planting of vineyards. It was difficult work because the terraces had to be supported with stones that were carried by hand and put in place. Any soil that was required in the terraces had to be carried on the shoulders of the men. It required great effort because they were steep slopes.

c) The time of harvest

The crop was planted in the spring. During the summer, the vines would be pruned. The branches would be tied down to produce the greatest amount of fruit. They would harvest the grapes near the end of September. It wasn't long after that that the rainy season began. So it was vital that the harvest be completed before the rains began. Harvest time was hectic. The owner knew he had to get his crop in. He needed more help beyond his regular servants, so he went to the village to hire day-laborers to help him harvest his crop.

3. The laborers identified

The laborers would gather in the town, usually at the marketplace (Gk., *agora*)—a common meeting place for day-laborers. There they would wait for anyone who might hire them. The owner of the estate showed up before 6:00 A.M. so he could hire them for a full day.

a) Their classification

What kind of laborers did the owner hire? In the society of Israel, there were people who owned land. Then there were those who were employed by the landowners on a long-term basis. Household servants and slaves would be included in this group. But the lowest class of people on the economic ladder were the day-laborers. They had no guarantee of work beyond the moment. They came to the marketplace every day, hoping they would be hired.

b) Their wage

The wage the day-laborer received was usually low. But they had to work for it because they were desperate just to have work. A Roman soldier was paid a denarius a day, and that was a respectable wage. Servants who were well-respected by their employers were often paid a denarius a day. But a day-laborer was usually hired for much less because he wasn't in any position to negotiate. If he didn't work, he didn't eat that day. He was barely able to provide for himself and his family.

God's Concern for the Day-Laborer

God's concern for such workers is clearly stated in two verses from the Old Testament:

1. Leviticus 19:13—"The wages of him that is hired shall not abide with thee all night until the morning." When a man was hired for a day, he needed to be paid at the end of the day.

2. Deuteronomy 24:15—"Thou shalt give him his hire, neither shall the sun go down upon it; for he is poor, and setteth his heart upon it; lest he cry against thee unto the Lord, and it be sin unto thee."

The day-laborers were on the bottom rung of the economic ladder. But the Lord included within the Levitical law the command that they be cared for properly. When they worked a day, they were to be paid a day's wage. If they didn't get paid, they couldn't eat that day. They weren't able to stockpile their resources. They were not self-sufficient apart from their daily labor.

B. The Laborers Hired (vv. 2-7)

1. The first group (v. 2)

Matthew 20:2 says, "When he had agreed with the laborers for a denarius a day, he sent them into his vineyard." The owner offered the laborers an honorable wage, one that was more than they would normally receive. The men agreed it was fair because they went to work for that amount.

2. The second group (vv. 3-4)

The owner "went out about the third hour [9:00 A.M.], and saw others standing idle in the market place, and said unto them, Go ye also into the vineyard, and whatever is right, I will give you. And they went their way" (vv. 3-4). When the owner went back to town, he found other men who were out of work. They weren't idle in terms of not wanting to work, otherwise they wouldn't have been gathered at the market place waiting for someone to hire them.

I get the feeling that the owner didn't need the workers as much as he was compassionate for their needs. He knew if they didn't work, they wouldn't eat. After finding them, he sent them into the field to work. Notice that he didn't negotiate a price with them. All he said was, "Whatever is right, I will give you" (v. 4). They took him at his word, knowing him to be an honorable man. They weren't in any position to negotiate—they had no choice but to take whatever they could get. Consequently, day-laborers often were taken advantage of. But apparently they trusted this man, so they went to work in the vineyard without an established wage.

3. The third and fourth groups (v. 5)

Matthew 20:5 says, "Again he went out about the sixth [noon] and ninth hour [3:00 P.M.], and did the same." The owner continued to go back to the marketplace and gathered more to work in his vineyard.

4. The last group (vv. 6-7)

The work day is almost gone when verse 6 says, "About the eleventh hour [5:00 P.M.] he went out, and found others standing idle." These workers had been waiting all day. By this time they would have been feeling depressed, realizing they would be providing no sustenance for their family that day. But the owner said to them, "Why stand ye here all the day idle? They say unto him, Because no man hath hired us" (vv. 6-7). Perhaps they had not been hired because they were older, weaker, or ignorant, but certainly not for their lack of desire. Then the owner said, "Go ye also into the vineyard, and whatever is right, that shall ye receive" (v. 7). You can be sure they ran to get in all the work they possibly could, knowing they were working without an established wage.

C. The Laborers Rewarded (vv. 8-15)

1. The generosity of the owner (vv. 8-9)

Verse 8 says, "So when evening was come [6:00 P.M.], the lord of the vineyard saith unto his steward, Call the laborers, and give them their hire." The owner was an honorable man—he was faithful to the commands in Leviticus and Deuteronomy to pay the laborers at the end of the day.

Then the owner added, "Beginning from the last unto the first" (v. 8). That intersects with our proverb. Those who came to work last were paid first, and the ones who came to work first were paid last. That is how the parable illustrates the proverb. The men in the front of the line worked one hour while those at the end of the line had worked twelve. Verse 9 says, "When they came that were hired about the eleventh hour, they received every man a denarius." That was a whole day's wage given for just one hour of work.

2. The grumblings of the last in line (vv. 10-12)

   a) Their false assumption (v. 10)

   You can imagine the men at the end of the line were saying, "Did you see that? He's paying a denarius an hour!" They thought by the time he got to them they'd receive twelve days' wages. Implied in the parable is that the 3:00 P.M., the noon, and the 9:00 A.M. groups received a denarius also. Verse 10 says, "But when the first came, they supposed that they should have received more; and they likewise received every man a denarius." Is that fair? Well, what had he promised to give them? A denarius (v. 2). And they believed it to be a fair wage.

   b) Their jealous murmurings (vv. 11-12)

   Matthew 20:11 says, "When they had received it, they murmured against the householder." The word translated "murmured" in the Greek text is *egogguzon*. It's onomatopoetic—the word is formed by the sound that is made. They grumbled and complained. In verse 12 they say, "These last have worked but one hour, and thou hast made them equal unto us, who have borne the burden and heat of the day." The owner wasn't unfair with them; it was just that he was generous with the rest. Some people have a hard time when others prosper. The issue here is not the fairness of the householder but the jealousy of those who worked the longest. Don't impugn God; impugn them. They received what was fair, but they were filled with envy, saying, "Thou hast made them equal unto us, who have borne the burden and heat of the day" (v. 12). The

Greek word translated "heat" is often used of the scorching east wind that would parch the lips and crack the skin. They graphically dramatized their plight. It is extremely hot in that part of the world at the end of September. If you have ever performed hard labor as they had, you can appreciate their situation. You could easily agree with their analysis.

3. The goodness of the owner

In Matthew 20:13 the owner answers one of them and calls him "friend." That is a translation of the Greek word *hetairos*, which is a nondescript term for a person. Then the owner said, "I do thee no wrong. Didst not thou agree with me for a denarius? Take what is thine, and go thy way; I will give unto this last, even as unto thee. Is it not lawful for me to do what I will with mine own? Is thine eye evil, because I am good?" (vv. 13-15).

An "evil eye" is jealousy. The evil eye resents what someone else has. Jealousy is a part of our fallen nature. The first laborers weren't upset over their wage because they knew it was a generous one. What they couldn't stand was someone else getting the same thing without working as hard as they had. They should have said, "Isn't it wonderful how generous the owner is to those who have the same need we have but weren't hired as early?"

D. The Proverb Repeated (v. 16)

Verse 16 says, "So the last shall be first, and the first last." The King James Version adds, "Many are called, but few chosen." The better manuscripts don't include that phrase. It seems to have been borrowed from Matthew 22:14.

III. THE POINT

What is the point of the parable? We understand that the owner paid all the laborers equally, whether they started early or late. So the last shall be first, and the first shall be last means everyone receives the same thing. The last laborers hired were the first in line to receive their wages, and the first were last in line to get the same wage. The point is equality. But what is the spiritual point? What does this parable teach about the kingdom?

A. The Commentary on the Parable

1. The interpretation

The householder represents God. The vineyard is the kingdom—the sphere of God's rule. The laborers are those who come into the service of the King. The day of work is their lifetime. The evening is eternity. The denarius is eternal life. You could say the steward represents Jesus Christ, to whom has been committed all judgment. So what does it all mean? No matter how long you worked in God's kingdom and no matter how hard or easy your circumstances were, when you get to the end of your life, you will receive the same eternal life as everyone else in God's kingdom. Isn't that a great truth?

2. The implications

Some Christians serve Christ almost their entire life, and some for a short time. You can imagine how those who worked the full twelve-hour day felt. They had worked in the hot sun while those who were hired at 5:00 P.M. worked when the breezes began at twilight. But that's how it is in God's kingdom. We all enter into the same eternal life. We all inherit the same glories in heaven.

Our Lord is teaching us that no matter how easy or hard our lot in life is and no matter how long or short our service, we will all receive the same spiritual blessings in the heavenlies. To put it another way, the penitent thief will inherit the same glories of eternity that belong to the apostles. Peter was crucified upside down for the cause of Christ. The penitent thief was crucified for his crimes. But both entered into eternal life to receive the same blessings. You may think that is inequitable, but it is more than any of us deserve. It is only by God's good pleasure that we are able to enter His kingdom. Those who come to Christ early in life will receive the same eternal life as those who come to Him late in life. Those who have not served Christ with a great amount of toil will receive the same eternal life as those who have served Christ to the point of dying a martyr's death. The benefits of the kingdom are the same for everyone as a result of God's grace and nothing else. That tells me we cannot earn our way into heaven. Entrance into the kingdom is not based on a merit system.

A pastor I know well related to me the circumstances that surrounded his father's death. His father lived his whole life as a Christ-rejecter, which was the opposite of his son, who had loved Christ and preached His gospel for years. His father suffered a stroke. While he lay in the hospital near death, no longer able to communicate, his son presented the gospel of Jesus Christ to him with all his heart. He told him how he could embrace Christ even at this point in his life, and even after rejecting Him for so many years. My friend told me, "I don't know whether he received Christ or not, but I did all I could to give him the message. And I have the confidence to know that if he believed, he'll inherit the same eternal life as I." That's a good illustration of what Jesus is teaching in the parable.

B. The Context of the Parable

1. The rejection of submission

    In Matthew 19:16-22, a rich young ruler comes to Jesus to find out how to get eternal life. Jesus told him how, but the ruler didn't want it because it meant making a sacrifice he wasn't willing to make.

2. The recipients of salvation

    In response to Christ's dialogue with the ruler, Peter speaks on behalf of the twelve disciples in verse 27: "Behold, we have forsaken all, and followed thee." They did what the young ruler wasn't willing to do. You could say that the disciples are in the 6:00 A.M. group. When Jesus began His ministry, He called the twelve first. So this parable is primarily directed to them. They were the ones who had been working through the heat of the day. They had been bearing that burden much longer than a twelve-hour day—it had been nearly three years. Since they had deprived themselves of a home and cut themselves off from former relationships, they wanted to know what they would receive for their sacrifice.

The disciples thought they were going to receive something special. I believe they loved Christ. I also am confident they believed He was the Messiah. They struggled with that idea at times, but they were genuine believers. However, connected with their genuineness was the idea that they were going to inherit the kingdom soon, and that excited them. They expected an earthly, political kingdom and all the glory and riches that would come with it. They thought that since they were the first group, they would sit at the right and left of the Messiah, calling the shots when the kingdom came. They believed Jesus was going to bring the kingdom at any minute. That's why they were so confused when it didn't happen. And you can imagine what must have been going through their minds when it looked like the entire prospect had collapsed at Christ's crucifixion. Even after Jesus rose from the dead and they met together, they still said, "Wilt thou at this time restore again the kingdom to Israel?" (Acts 1:6). They expected to get their crowns and thrones right then. They were looking for something special for themselves.

3. The requirement of suffering

In Matthew 20:17, which immediately follows the parable, Jesus is going to Jerusalem with the disciples. He then pulled them aside away from the crowd to explain their purpose for going there. He says, "We go up to Jerusalem; and the Son of man shall be betrayed unto the chief priests and unto the scribes, and they shall condemn him to death, and shall deliver him to the Gentiles to mock, and to scourge, and to crucify him. And the third day he shall rise again" (vv. 18-19). Jesus tells them He was not going to Jerusalem to set up the kingdom but to die. The disciples didn't understand that.

4. The request of selfish men

   a) The instigation of the two disciples

   Matthew 20:20-21 says, "Then came to him the mother of Zebedee's children with her sons [James and John], worshiping him, and desiring a certain thing of him. And he said unto her, What wilt thou? She saith unto him, Grant that these, my two sons, may sit, the one on thy right hand, and the other on the left, in thy kingdom." When you think about the apostle John, you usually picture a gentle, sensitive, and humble man. And you can conceive of James as someone who was willing to be all that the Lord wanted him to be. But they wanted to be important in the kingdom.

   The disciples were constantly arguing about who would be the greatest in the kingdom. When Jesus washed their feet in the upper room the night before His death, they argued about it (Luke 22:24). That's why no one thought about washing the others' feet before the meal. None of them wanted to take the role of a servant and be disqualified from being the greatest. They all wanted to be the head man next to Jesus. So Jesus girded His loins and washed their feet Himself (John 13:4-5).

   James and John were so hungry for the chief seats in the kingdom that they brought their mother to appeal to Jesus. They remembered He had told them that "in the regeneration, when the Son of man shall sit on the throne of his glory, ye shall also sit upon twelve thrones, judging the twelve tribes of Israel" (Matt. 19:28). James and John interpreted that to mean there would be a throne on His right and one on His left. They were self-centered. Jesus told them that they wouldn't be able to handle what He was going to have to go through, and that only the Father could give those seats to them (Matt. 20:23).

b) The indignation of the ten disciples

Verse 24 says, "When the ten heard it, they were moved with indignation against the two brethren." Why? Because they thought James and John might get something they wouldn't. They were upset because they wanted the seats next to Christ. You can imagine what the kingdom would have been like had they all entered with those attitudes. They would have made mad dashes to get the inside seats.

Jesus probably grew tired of their quibbling about what they thought they might get as a result of their sacrifice in following Him. So Jesus taught them about being humble: "Whosoever will be great among you, let him be your minister" (v. 26). Jesus isn't looking for people who want the chief seats, but for those who will serve like the Son of man, who "came not to be ministered unto, but to minister, and to give His life a ransom for many" (v. 28).

5. The restoration of sinners

After Jesus taught them about service, they came across two blind men as they left Jericho. Blind men were outcasts in that society. Many were forced to line the roads and beg for money to support themselves. As Jesus passed they said, "Have mercy on us, O Lord, thou Son of David. And the multitude rebuked them, that they should hold their peace; but they cried the more, saying, Have mercy on us, O Lord, thou Son of David. And Jesus stood still, and called them, and said, What will ye that I should do unto you? They say unto Him, Lord, that our eyes may be opened. So Jesus had compassion on them, and touched their eyes; and immediately their eyes received sight, and they followed him" (vv. 30-34). You can well imagine that the disciples did not consider those two blind beggars as being in the same class as themselves. That was the attitude Jesus wanted to correct. The blind beggars came to Christ later than the disciples. In a short time Jesus was going to die. What did they endure? They were like the laborers who were hired at 5:00 P.M. and worked for an hour in the cool of the day. It didn't seem that they had to pay a high price to get into the kingdom.

C. The Conclusion of the Parable

1. Equal salvation for all

The Lord was attempting to deal with the selfish, indulgent, envious, and confused perception of the disciples with the parable of the laborers. He was saying, "Salvation is not earned; it is a gift I give according to My sovereign will. It is not a question of when you came in, how long you worked, how hot the trials were, or how hard you worked." There is nothing mentioned in the parable about how hard anyone worked.

Jesus is going to give the same reward to everyone who knows Him. However, we often think in the same way as the disciples, saying, "I've served the Lord through many trials. I've suffered through great pain." Yet we all will receive the same eternal life. Tax collectors, harlots, beggars, and blind people will share in the same eternal life as those who served their entire life or were martyred for the cause of Christ. We all will be blessed with all spiritual blessings in the heavenlies in Christ Jesus because that's the way God wants it.

2. Equal inheritance for all

When we get to heaven, we'll all live in the Father's house. Jesus said, "In my Father's house are many mansions" (John 14:2). We're all the bride of Christ (2 Cor. 11:2). None of us are just guests at the wedding. Romans 8:17 says we are "heirs of God, and joint heirs with Christ." The Roman inheritance was different than the Jewish inheritance. The heads of Jewish families gave a double portion to the older son, but the heads of Roman families gave equal inheritance to all members. And that is the kind of inheritance Paul was referring to in Romans 8:17, only with greater significance because we don't each receive an equal part; we each receive the whole.

The Ultimate Reward

Now you might bring up the subject of rewards at this point, for certainly the epistles tell us that we will receive rewards for our service to Christ. But that is a different issue because here Jesus is discussing the equal nature of eternal life.

The Lord will be pleased to give His children different rewards according to their service. I don't know what those rewards are, but I can't imagine anything better than everlasting life. Once you've received that, how could you have anything more wonderful? There are degrees of punishment in hell, but everything in hell is typified by the absence of God. You can't have more or less of the absence of God. And if you have everlasting life, you can't have more or less everlasting life. I don't understand what God's rewards will be like; I just know He gives the same eternal life to all believers. He makes no distinction between male and female, rich and poor, or Jew and Greek (Gal. 3:28).

IV. THE PRINCIPLES

A. God Initiates Salvation

In the parable, the householder went out to find the laborers and bring them into his vineyard. God goes into the marketplace of the world to seek those who would serve in His kingdom. Since God does the seeking and the saving, we have no right to put demands on what we ought to get. If He happened to seek and save us early so that we have our whole life to serve Him, that is His choice. If we are saved late so that we have just a brief time to serve Him, that too is His choice.

B. God Establishes the Terms of Salvation

The householder told the first laborers that he would give them a denarius. He set the price, and they agreed to those terms. The rich young ruler didn't agree to pay the price Christ set. But the day-laborers were so poor and in need that they willingly came on the householder's terms. When he approached the other groups of laborers, he told them he would pay them what was right, and they came on those terms. They didn't argue.

C. God Continues to Call Men into His Kingdom

I believe the reason that laborers were hired at different hours is to show us that all through man's day God is calling people into His kingdom. It is an ongoing work. In John 9:4 Jesus says, "I must work the works of him that sent me, while it is day; the night cometh, when no man can work." Redemption continues on until the judgment comes.

D. God Redeems Those Who Are Willing

The men who were looking for work needed someone to care for them. They were not rich, self-sufficient, or complacent. They were poor and meek, begging for work. Those without resources came to the master for what they could get only from him. Those are the kind of people who are saved—those who in the last hour of life still have no resources. It is only through the compassion of the owner who gives the denarius that they are saved. We don't know why the householder didn't hire all the men in the morning. But neither do we know why God saves people at different stages of life. We do know that the need is always there. It is His sovereignty that determines when He will come to those whose hearts are willing because they lack resources.

E. God Is Compassionate Toward Those Who Have No Resources

God reaches out to those who recognize their need. The householder asked the laborers why they were idle. They said to him, "Because no one will hire us. We want to do the right thing, but no one will provide for us. We want sustenance, we want bread and food, but we don't have anyone to give it to us." It is those kind of people the Lord reaches out to.

F. God Saves Those Who Are Willing to Work

All who came into the householder's vineyard worked. Some may have come in at the last hour, but they worked. I don't see any freeloaders in the group. Some worked a short time and some worked a long time, but they all worked. And that's the way it is in salvation: your faith is known by your works (James 2:18).

G. God Keeps His Promise

The householder told the first group he would give them a denarius. I believe that illustrates that God never gives less than He promises. When some of us came to Christ, we knew well what was prepared for us of the fullness of eternal life. We had been instructed in the gospel or raised in the church. There may be others of us who came to Christ in desperation—in a situation where there was no price to negotiate. Maybe we came to Him later on in life when we were desperate because we needed sustenance. But whatever He wants to give us is enough.

H. God Gives More Than We Deserve

The householder gave the other groups of laborers, who did not work a full day, more than they deserved. Everything we receive is of grace.

I. God Requires Humility

We need to have a sense of unworthiness. There is no room for jealousy—no place for thinking I ought to have more in glory than you ought to have. There is no room for my acting the part of the older brother in the story of the prodigal son (Luke 15:11-32). The younger brother lived a wild life, wasted all his substance, and wound up in a pig pen. He finally came home, repented, and embraced his father. The father killed the fatted calf, put a ring on his son's finger, put a robe on him, and had a celebration for him. What was the older brother doing? Complaining. Why? Because he didn't get a fatted calf? He could have had all the fatted calves he wanted. Because he didn't get a ring? He could have had all the rings he wanted. Because he didn't get a robe? He probably had many robes in his closet. He was complaining because he didn't think his brother deserved what he got.

You may say, "I've been faithful in the church. I haven't blown my life. I know of other Christians who left the church but then the Lord accepted them back. Surely in heaven there will be more for me." No. That's the older-brother mentality. That attitude has nothing to do with the equality of grace, but it has a lot to do with the jealousy of men.

J. God Is Gracious

All we receive from God is a matter of His grace. Our works bring nothing to bear on our salvation. God dispenses His sovereign grace to all who come into His vineyard, no matter how long or how short they work, or how hard or easy the work seems. God gives the same eternal life to all who trust in Him. The equalizer is grace, because where sin abounds, grace much more abounds (Rom. 5:20). I think that's what the apostle Paul is referring to when he says to the Ephesians: "God, who is rich in mercy, for his great love with which he loved us, even when we were dead in sins, hath made us alive together with Christ (by grace ye are saved), and hath raised us up together, and hath made us sit together in heavenly places in Christ Jesus; that in the ages to come he might show the exceeding riches of his grace in his kindness toward us through Christ Jesus" (Eph. 2:4-7). God wants to forever give us the fullness of all that eternal life is, and that's why He redeemed us.

God treats everyone equally. When we enter His kingdom, His grace allows us all to inherit the same eternal life. The parable of the laborers wonderfully exalts God's grace and eliminates any thought man might have of attaining eternal life on his own.

Focusing on the Facts

1. What was one of the principle duties for God's spokesmen (see p. 50)?
2. What does the phrase "God is no respecter of persons" mean (see p. 51)?
3. What is a proverb (see p. 52)?
4. What is the meaning of the proverb in Matthew 19:30 and 20:16 (see p. 53)?
5. Why do we need an earthly illustration to teach us a spiritual lesson (see p. 53)?

6. Describe the householder (see p. 53).

7. What kind of laborers did the householder hire? Describe them (see p. 55).

8. What kind of wage did the householder offer the first group of laborers? What kind of wage did he offer the other laborers (see pp. 56-57?

9. What event in the parable intersects with the proverb in Matthew 19:30 and 20:16 (Matt. 20:8; see p. 57)?

10. What was the false assumption of the first group of laborers (see p. 58)?

11. What were the first group of laborers really complaining about (see p. 58)?

12. What do the various people and things represent in the parable of the laborers (see p. 60)?

13. What is the spiritual point of the parable (see p. 60)?

14. To whom was Jesus' parable primarily directed (see p. 61)?

15. What kind of expectations did the disciples hold for the kingdom (see p. 62)?

16. What reason did Jesus give for going to Jerusalem (Matt. 20:17-19; see p. 62)?

17. What did James and John desire for themselves? Why were the other ten disciples angry with James and John (Matt. 20:20-24; see pp. 63-64)?

18. What kind of people is Jesus looking for to enter His kingdom (see p. 64)?

19. Describe how the Roman inheritance was different from the Jewish inheritance. How does the inheritance God gives His children differ from both (Rom. 8:17; see p. 65)?

Pondering the Principles

1. Have you ever accused God of being unequal in His treatment of people? Give some examples. From this study we have learned that God treats everyone equally. But what about your treatment of others? Do you treat everyone equally? Read James 2:1-13. Analyze your treatment of others in light of this passage. What changes can you put into practice today?

2. The first laborers were envious of the last group because they received the same pay. The Bible has a lot to say about envy. Look up the following verses: Proverbs 14:30; Romans 13:13-14; and James 3:14-16; 4:1-4. Based on those verses, what have you

learned about envy? According to James 3:17-18 and 4:7-10, how can you overcome the sin of envy? Commit yourself to follow the suggestions of James to deal with any envious attitudes you have.

3. Review the principles we can learn from the parable of the laborers (see pp. 66-69). Which ones deal with things God does for us? Which ones deal with our responses to God? Think back on the circumstances involving your salvation. How did those principles apply in your circumstances? Don't forget all that God has done for you in giving you salvation. Draw near to Him right now, and thank Him for His grace.

4
The Sufferings of Christ

Outline

Introduction
A. The Propositions of the Rejecters
B. The Plan of the Savior

Lesson
I. The Plan of His Sufferings
  A. The Faithfulness of Christ
    1. His movement toward Jerusalem
    2. His message to the disciples
      a) The commitment of Christ
      b) The confusion of the disciples
        (1) They were amazed
        (2) They were afraid
  B. The Focus of the Old Testament
    1. The specific predictions
    2. The sweeping picture
      a) A sacrifice is a covering
      b) A sacrifice is a substitute
      c) A sacrifice is pure
      d) Sacrifice is a way of life
  C. The Fulfillment of the Plan
    1. The affirmation of Christ
    2. The affirmation of Scripture
      a) 1 Corinthians 15:3-4
      b) 1 Peter 1:11
      c) Luke 2:25-35
      d) John 1:29
      e) Revelation 5:5-6

Introduction

Matthew 20:17-19 says, "Jesus, going up to Jerusalem, took the twelve disciples aside along the way, and said unto them, Behold, we go up to Jerusalem; and the Son of man shall be betrayed unto the chief priests and unto the scribes, and they shall condemn him to death, and shall deliver him to the Gentiles to mock, and to scourge, and to crucify him. And the third day he shall rise again."

There is no question about what Christ means. It is the third and last prediction of our Lord regarding His death and resurrection. He gave the first to the disciples in Matthew 16:21 and the second in Matthew 17:22-23. The second added detail to the first, and this one adds detail to the second.

The death and resurrection of Jesus Christ is the center of biblical revelation. It is the most important Christian truth. The theme of this particular announcement, however, takes us beyond the earlier two. Whereas they talked about only His death and resurrection, this one stresses the nature and details of His suffering. He explains in detail that He will be betrayed and handed over to the chief priests and scribes. They will condemn Him to death and then hand Him over to the pagans. They in turn will mock, scourge, and finally crucify Him. After that Christ will rise from the dead. So the theme of this particular prediction by our Lord is His sufferings.

A. The Propositions of the Rejecters

Some rejecters of the truth have tried to categorize Jesus Christ as totally human and not deity. Some have said He was a well-meaning, loving, gentle, and peaceful individual who somehow got caught in a hostile world and was accidentally crucified. Others have been less generous and said He was a self-styled, would-be conqueror who tried to pull off a coup only to end up a victim of His own revolution. There are many other propositions in between.

B. The Plan of the Savior

The sufferings of Jesus Christ were no accident or miscalculation. He was able to give in exact detail all that was going to happen to Him. Among His first recorded words are these: "I must be about my Father's business" (Luke 2:49). Just before His death He said, "It is finished" (John 19:30). It is obvious He knew what He was supposed to do and when He had finished it. That Jesus knew every single detail of His sufferings indicates to me He must have suffered through them a thousand times before He actually endured them. Being omniscient, He was able to conceive of all that His suffering would be.

I believe Jesus wanted the disciples to understand His sufferings. They anticipated the glories of the kingdom and the Messiah—those prophecies they seemed to understand quite well. They didn't understand that the Messiah had to suffer first. But we shouldn't be too hard on them for their ignorance. Even with all that they know today, the Jewish people still don't understand. The disciples were looking for a lion; they didn't know they needed a lamb. But Jesus knew. So He called them aside for the third time and told them once more.

Lesson

I. THE PLAN OF HIS SUFFERINGS

A. The Faithfulness of Christ

Matthew 20:17-18 says, "Jesus, going up to Jerusalem, took the twelve disciples aside along the way, and said unto them, Behold, we go up to Jerusalem." Based on the words Jesus chose to use, one gets the feeling He knew well what He was doing. The word *behold* indicates a certain amount of surprise, as if to say, "It may seem startling to you, and you may not understand it, but we are going to Jerusalem." There's a resolution and conviction in His statement. Luke 9:51 says, "He steadfastly set his face to go to Jerusalem." Jesus was resolute in His commitment.

1. His movement toward Jerusalem

As He finished His ministry in the northern part of Galilee, Jesus crossed the Jordan in the north and traveled east of the Jordan to an area known as Peraea. He worked His way south through Peraea and down the Jordan. Matthew 19 and the first part of chapter 20 give us incidents in that ministry. Then He crossed the Jordan once more as He moved toward Jerusalem. On His way He would go through Jericho (Matt. 20:29). It was from there that He would begin His long ascent to Jerusalem. It was only a matter of days until He would face His death and resurrection.

Notice that Matthew 20:18 says, "We go up to Jerusalem." Jesus and the disciples literally had to go up. Jericho is about one thousand feet below sea level, and Jerusalem is well over five thousand feet above sea level. Yet they're no more than fifteen miles apart. So we're talking about a steep ascent.

You can imagine that Jesus and the disciples weren't alone. The Peraean ministry had no doubt caused a mass of people to congregate around them. Matthew 20:29 says, "As they departed from Jericho, a great multitude followed him." Since this was Passover time, there would normally be a large crowd traveling to Jerusalem. But this crowd had an added attraction because they found themselves in the company of Jesus, the astounding teacher and healer. So as was typical in His Galilean ministry, we find Jesus once more surrounded by a multitude of people.

2. His message to the disciples

   a) The commitment of Christ

   While on the way to Jerusalem, Jesus again felt a need to communicate to His disciples about what was going to happen. So He pulled them aside somewhere away from the crowd to speak to them. He said to them, "We go up to Jerusalem." It may have sounded shocking and strange to the disciples, but that was exactly where they were going.

   b) The confusion of the disciples

   Mark gives us a parallel account to Matthew 20:17-19. Mark 10:32 says that the disciples were both amazed and afraid. Why? Because they knew the hostility of the Jerusalem aristocracy. They knew that both the chief priests and scribes were enemies of Christ. They had already experienced many conflicts with the Pharisees. They couldn't see any purpose in going to Jerusalem. They also knew that the Roman seat was there. Perhaps they felt that if they were ever going to pull off a revolution, they ought to start it in Galilee and let it become an ascending grass-roots revolution. They realized that a motley group of thirteen wouldn't be able to take over a city the size of Jerusalem. So they were somewhat confused.

   Mark 10:32 also says that Jesus walked in front of the disciples. He was like a commander leading his troops into battle, putting Himself in the most dangerous and vulnerable position. To me, there are few pictures in the gospels that are more striking. Je-

sus steadfastly moved toward His death on behalf of
His disciples. Their anticipation of the kingdom
mingled with their fear of death.

(1) They were amazed

The Greek word translated "amazed" in Mark
10:32 is *thambeō*. Its use in the Bible is rare: three
times in Mark and once in Acts 9:6. Based on
those four uses and the queries that result from
each, it seems to me that the best way to trans-
late it is "to be confused" or "to be baffled." It is
not the amazement of seeing something wonderful and awesome; it is the confusion and chaos of the mind that comes when you can't make
sense out of what is happening. That's exactly
what Paul experienced when he became blind on
the road to Damascus as he was confronted by
the resurrected Christ (Acts 9:6). And that's how
Mark uses it.

(2) They were afraid

As a result of their confusion, they were afraid.
The Greek word Mark uses for "afraid" is *phobos*,
from which we get the word *phobia*. The disciples
experienced anxiety because of their confusion
over Jesus' desire to go to Jerusalem when He
knew full well that the leaders hated Him and
wanted to take His life. But Jesus remained resolute because it was the divine plan, and He
wanted to get on with it.

B. The Focus of the Old Testament

In the parallel passage in Luke 18:31 Jesus says, "Behold,
we go up to Jerusalem, and all things that are written by
the prophets concerning the Son of man shall be accom-
plished." Jesus had to go to Jerusalem because it was the
prophetic plan. His suffering was no accident. It was not a
bad turn in a nice revolution; it was foretold by myriad
prophets. People who accuse Jesus of being some mis-
guided patriot or some well-meaning peacemaker whose

revolution went awry not only misunderstand Jesus but misunderstand the Old Testament as well. They simply demonstrate their ignorance. Jesus' sufferings were the culmination of the redemptive plan of God.

1. The specific predictions

There are many passages in the Old Testament that predict all the factors of the Messiah's life.

a) Zechariah 9:9 says He will enter into Jerusalem.

b) Psalm 2:1-3 says He will know the fury and rage of His enemies.

c) Zechariah 13:7 says He will be deserted by His friends.

d) Zechariah 11:12 says He will be betrayed for thirty pieces of silver.

e) Psalm 22:14-17 says He will be crucified.

f) Psalm 34:20 says none of His bones will be broken (cf. Ex. 12:46).

g) Psalm 22:18 says His garments will be parted by the casting of lots.

h) Psalm 69:21 says He will be given vinegar to drink.

i) Psalm 22:1 says He will cry out in pain of distress.

j) Zechariah 12:10 says they will pierce Him with a spear.

k) Psalm 16:10 says He will rise from the dead.

l) Psalm 110:1 says He will ascend into heaven.

All those predictions are part of the Old Testament prophecies. A detailed description of the suffering and death of Jesus Christ can be seen in Psalm 22, Isaiah 53, and Zechariah 12. So as He went to Jerusalem, Jesus remained on schedule with no deviation.

2. The sweeping picture

The whole sweep of the Old Testament, in its types, symbols, and pictures, demands that the Messiah die for the sins of the world. The death of Jesus Christ is the primary event in history. It is the scarlet thread woven throughout Scripture.

a) A sacrifice is a covering

Immediately after Adam and Eve sinned in Genesis 3:6, they knew they were now separated from God. So the first thing they did was hide themselves from Him. They became aware that they were naked. In verse 21 God clothes them with the skins of animals, which had to die. We see that guilt, shame, and separation are covered by a sacrifice. This passage is not a verbal prediction about Jesus Christ, but it sets in motion a truth that demands the ultimate Passover Lamb.

b) A sacrifice is a substitute

God gave Abraham a son named Isaac, in whom all his hopes resided. From him would come a generation of people numbering as the sand of the sea and the stars of heaven (Gen. 22:17). But God told Abraham to kill his son, which would mean the death of Abraham's hopes and God's promises. Yet Abraham remained faithful and committed himself to do what God said. So he loaded wood on Isaac's back, and they started up the hill of sacrifice known as Mount Moriah (v. 6). When they reached the top, Abraham "built an altar there, laid the wood in order, and bound Isaac, his son, and laid him on the altar upon the wood" (v. 9). At the moment Abraham lifted the knife to drive it into the heart of his son, God stopped him. Then Abraham saw a ram caught in a thicket. He then sacrificed the ram in place of Isaac (vv. 10-13).

According to Hebrews 11:19, Abraham's faith was sustained in that he believed God would raise Isaac from the dead. That's how much he believed God would keep His promise. So when God held Abraham's hand and provided a ram, we see that God will provide a substitute. Genesis 22:14 says that Abraham named the place of sacrifice Jehovah-jireh, "The Lord will provide." We learn that sin, shame, and guilt can be dealt with only by a sacrifice that God provides.

c) A sacrifice is pure

God said He would send the angel of death throughout Egypt to slay the first born of every house (Ex. 11:5). So that the Israelites would be protected, God commanded Moses to tell the people to sacrifice an unblemished lamb (Ex. 12:3-5). They were to put the blood on the doorposts and lintel of their homes (v. 7). The angel of death, upon seeing the blood, would pass by that house (v. 13). So the people were delivered from judgment by making a blood sacrifice. That repeats what we learned in Genesis 3; sin has to be dealt with by sacrifice. It also repeats what we learned in Genesis 22; a sacrifice can be substituted for a guilty person. Now a third dimension is added to redemptive truth: the sacrifice must be unblemished—it must be pure.

d) Sacrifice is a way of life

When the nation of Israel left Egypt, they began their wanderings in the wilderness at Sinai. God brought all the people together and gave Moses His law. God then began to unfold through Moses all the intricate elements of the sacrificial system. Sacrifice then became a way of life for the people. Every day, every national feast, and every act of worship was based on a sacrifice.

There can be no worship of God without sacrifice. That is why the first of five offerings was the burnt offering (Lev. 1). The sacrifice in its entirety was offered to God and wasn't used to support the priests in any way.

81

C. The Fulfillment of the Plan

God had to provide an unblemished sacrifice who could redeem His people and provide the kind of sacrifice that could open up the way of true worship forever. That's why the veil of the Temple was torn away when Jesus died on the cross (Matt. 27:51). The sacrificial system was over because Jesus was the one final sacrifice who opened the pathway to God. We can now worship without ever having to offer another bloody sacrifice.

The Lord told the disciples that they all were going to Jerusalem. The disciples figured they were going there for the Passover, but they didn't know they were going there with the Passover Lamb. They were thinking *kingdom;* Jesus was thinking *sacrifice.* They were thinking *glory;* He was thinking *suffering.* When Peter, James, and John were on the mount of transfiguration with Christ, I'm sure they thought the kingdom had come to earth (Matt. 17:2-4). But they came down that mountain. Now Jesus was going to Jerusalem, so they became confused and afraid.

1. The affirmation of Christ

Jesus remained on schedule. Several places in the gospel of John, Jesus says, "I came to do the will of My Father." After His resurrection He met two disciples on the road to Emmaus and said to them, "Ought not Christ to have suffered these things, and to enter into his glory?" (Luke 24:26). I think He probably gave them a lesson similar to the one I just gave you. He probably took them through the writings and the flow of the Old Testament to show them the importance of sacrificial death. Luke 24:46 says, "Thus it is written, and thus it behooved Christ to suffer." People couldn't understand that He had to suffer.

2. The affirmation of Scripture

a) 1 Corinthians 15:3-4—Paul said, "Christ died for our sins . . . was buried, and . . . rose again the third day according to the scriptures."

82

b) 1 Peter 1:11—The prophets were "searching what, or what manner of time the Spirit of Christ who was in them did signify, when he testified beforehand the sufferings of Christ, and the glory that should follow." If you don't see both of those things in Christ, you have missed God's plan. That's why the Jewish people as a whole have missed Jesus as their Messiah; all they can see is the glory, and they don't understand His suffering. They don't know what to do with Psalm 22, Isaiah 53, and Zechariah 12. If you don't see the need for the suffering of Christ, you can't understand Him.

c) Luke 2:25-35—When Jesus was brought as a little child to the Temple by His mother, they met a devout man of God named Simeon (v. 25). He was waiting for the consolation of Israel. The Holy Spirit had revealed to him that he would not die until he saw the Messiah. When Jesus was brought into the Temple, Simeon picked Him up in his arms and blessed Him, saying, "Behold, this child is set for the fall and rising again of many in Israel; and for a sign which shall be spoken against" (v. 34). He then said to Mary, "Yea, a sword shall pierce through thy own soul also" (v. 35). Jesus' life would not be without pain and suffering. Only a mother's heart could know the suffering that Mary went through.

d) John 1:29—When John the Baptist saw Christ, he said, "Behold the Lamb of God, who taketh away the sin of the world."

e) Revelation 5:5-6—Christ is described as a lamb that was slain in verse 6. But verse 5 refers to Him as the Lion of the tribe of Judah.

II. THE PREDICTIONS OF HIS SUFFERINGS

In Matthew 20:18-19 Christ predicts in great detail what will happen to Him. But how did He know all that? There's only One who could know that, and it is God. Jesus Christ is God in human flesh. He was no ordinary man. He knew how many husbands a certain woman had even though He had never met her before. He even told her that the man she was living with wasn't her husband (John 4:18). He told His disciples to get the foal of a donkey and told them what would be said when they asked the owner for the animal (Luke 19:29-33). The phrase "the Son of man" is used some eighty times in the gospels. It's a term that refers to His humiliation, but it also incorporates His exaltation (Dan. 7:13).

A. Christ Was Betrayed to the Leaders

First, Jesus said He would be betrayed. The Greek verb for "betrayed" is not in Matthew 20:18. The word used means "to be handed over." But it is obvious that it implies betrayal. Judas turned Him over to the Jewish leaders, thus betraying Him.

1. The chief priests

The chief priests were the upper echelon among all the priests. The Levites were at the bottom. Next in line were the priests who served as treasurers. Above them were those who served as the Temple overseers. They were preceded by the priests who were the directors of the daily course (division) of priests. Above them were those who served as directors of the weekly course of priests. Then came the priest who served as the captain of the Temple. At the top was the high priest. The chief priests formed an independent body from the rest of the priesthood and dealt with affairs of the Temple and the priesthood. They were the aristocracy. They obtained their position through heredity.

2. The scribes

The chief priests were accompanied by the scribes, who obtained their rank by knowledge. They attained this knowledge by their study of the law. No one could interpret anything without them. Today, if you want to interpret any kind of law or be represented in any legal situation, you need a lawyer. The same thing was true then. In trying to interpret the Mosaic economy, the leaders needed to have lawyers. The scribes served that function. They would explain and interpret the meaning of the law.

B. Christ Was Condemned to Death

The chief priests and scribes made up the executive body of the Temple priesthood that ultimately condemned Jesus Christ to death, because He so threatened the security of their system. Jesus knew He would be betrayed to them. The priests rejected Christ. They were in a position to pull off a mock trial and condemn Him to death. That was no surprise to Him.

C. Christ Was Given to the Gentiles

The Jewish leaders couldn't kill Jesus because the Romans had removed their right to execute people. So they had to give Him over to the Gentiles, which they did after they brought some false charges against Him. Ultimately the charge was that He spoke against Caesar (John 19:12). Pontius Pilate, the Roman governor, couldn't find anything wrong with Him, but he finally succumbed to crucifying Him because of pressure from the Jewish leaders. They told Pilate they would tell Caesar if he didn't. Pilate already had many strikes against him in his relations with the Jews. If one more had occurred, the emperor probably would have removed Pilate from his position, and perhaps even have him killed.

When Jesus was taken to Fort Antonia, the following happened:

1. He was mocked

   Roman soldiers put a reed in His hand, jammed a crown of thorns on His head, spit all over Him, and jeered at Him.

2. He was scourged

   Next He was scourged. They lacerated His back with leather thongs that held bits of bone and metal at the ends. Then they laughed at Him in scorn.

3. He was crucified

   Ultimately, the Romans crucified Him. But He rose from the dead.

III. THE PROPORTION OF HIS SUFFERINGS

The one thing that stood out to me as I read over Matthew 20:17-19 was the amount of detail Jesus gave regarding His suffering. So I began to look through the Word of God to see what I could learn about Christ's sufferings. I found out that His sufferings are referred to in the plural (e.g., 2 Cor. 1:5; Phil. 3:10; Heb. 2:10; 1 Pet. 1:11; 4:13). Jesus' suffering was not one-dimensional. The proportion of His suffering was beyond anything I had ever thought about.

Many of us limit our perception of Christ's suffering to the nails driven through His hands, the spear thrust through His side, or the crown of thorns jammed on His head. There is little question that those things brought a great deal of suffering. First century Jewish historian Josephus tells of three men who were crucified. They were left until they should have been dead, but two of them lived. So crucifixion by itself doesn't always kill its victims. That is why the executioners would scourge those whom they especially wanted to die. The resulting blood loss and exposure of the internal organs, coupled with the pain involved, would make death inevitable.

There was much more to the suffering of Christ than just His physical suffering on the cross. Our bodies have an amazing ability to cope with shock and trauma. So I attempted to study all the facets of His suffering.

The Suffering Servant of Isaiah

Isaiah 53 reveals the proportion of Christ's sufferings quite clearly.

1. Verse 2—"He hath no form nor comeliness, and when we shall see him, there is no beauty that we should desire him." He suffered from being ugly and being rejected.

2. Verse 3—"We hid as it were our faces from Him; he was despised." Jesus suffered the sorrow of grief and the lack of esteem and respect. He suffered the internal pain of being despised and rejected. Remember that Jesus, God in human flesh, was never worthy of that kind of suffering.

3. Verse 4—"Surely he hath borne our griefs, and carried our sorrows." Sometimes we suffer more when we carry the pain of others than we do our own. The text then says, "We did esteem him stricken, smitten of God, and afflicted." He received blows from God's wrath that made Him cry out, "My God, My God, why hast thou forsaken me?" (Matt. 27:46).

4. Verse 5—"He was wounded for our transgressions, he was bruised for our iniquities; the chastisement for our peace was upon him, and with his stripes we are healed."

5. Verse 6—"All we like sheep have gone astray; we have turned every one to his own way, and the Lord hath laid on him the iniquity of us all." Here Christ is pictured alone, bearing all the sins of the world—a cosmic kind of divine loneliness.

6. Verse 7—"He was oppressed, and he was afflicted, yet he opened not his mouth." He didn't even defend Himself. He didn't say, "Stop, I'm the Son of God. I will not take this!" He had to suffer in absolute silence (cf. Matt. 27:12-14). So He experienced the suffering that comes with knowing that you're right, holy, and good.

7. Verse 8—"He was taken from prison and from [false] judgment. . . . He was cut off from the land of the living; for the transgression of my people was he stricken." That was the kind of suffering that preceded His death.

8. Verse 9—"He made his grave with the wicked." He suffered from being counted as a common criminal in His burial. He suffered even though "he had done no violence, neither was any deceit in his mouth."

9. Verse 10—"Yet it pleased the Lord to bruise him." Jesus suffered in knowing that it pleased God to do all those things to Him.

10. Verse 11—"He shall see of the travail of his soul." He suffered the pain of the soul.

11. Verse 12—"He hath poured out his soul unto death; and he was numbered with the transgressors; and he bore the sins of many." That is the sum of it all.

It is overwhelming to conceive of the proportion of the sufferings of our Lord. And I think that was on His heart as He went up the hill to Jerusalem.

A. Emotional Suffering

1. Disloyalty

Jesus suffered the pain of disloyalty in knowing He would soon be betrayed. Remember, much of this suffering came in anticipation of the event. Since He knew it was going to happen, He suffered the pain before it happened. In Psalm 41:9 the psalmist says, "Mine own familiar friend, in whom I trusted, who did eat of my bread, hath lifted up his heel against me." Jesus loved Judas; He walked and talked with him for three years and affirmed His love for him. Yet Judas betrayed Him with a kiss. So Christ suffered the betrayal of one who violated the intimacy of friendship.

2. Rejection

Jesus was turned over to the chief priests and scribes, and they condemned Him to death. The apostle John said, "He came unto his own, and his own received him not" (John 1:11). Jesus looked over the city of Jerusalem and wept, saying, "How often would I have gathered thy children together, even as a hen gathereth her chickens under her wings, and ye would not!" (Matt. 23:37). The leaders rejected Him. Isaiah said He was despised and rejected of men (Isa. 53:3). He was the cornerstone the builders rejected (1 Pet. 2:7). The people of His own nation—those He healed and taught—rejected Him. That heartbreak alone would be enough to kill a person. He was betrayed by a friend and rejected by His people. I believe that in all He suffered, He died of a broken heart.

But Jesus was rejected not only by men but also by God. Remember that He said, "My God, My God, why hast thou forsaken me?" (Matt. 27:46). In addition, Matthew 26:56 says, "All the disciples forsook him, and fled." Jesus didn't have anyone left. He was rejected by the people, by the disciples, and by God.

3. Humiliation

Notice that Matthew 20:19 says they mocked Him. They pulled at His beard, crammed a crown of thorns on His head, stuck a reed in His hand, put a robe on Him, and called Him a king. They spit on His face. They mocked, scorned, and ridiculed Him. Then they nailed Him to a cross naked before the whole world. The glorious, sinless Son of God was humiliated when He should have been exalted. Yet He never retaliated (1 Pet. 2:23). I can't imagine what it would have been like for Him to suffer such humiliation.

4. Injustice

The Romans scourged and crucified Him because He had been condemned. He was held responsible for something He was not guilty of. If any of us were accused of something we weren't guilty of, and it demanded a severe penalty, we would scream bloody murder! But in silence Christ was obliged to accept the responsibility for sins He never committed (Isa. 53:7). All the guilt of all the people who ever lived was put on Him. I can't imagine anything more terrible than to be put to death for a crime you knew you hadn't committed.

Those four things alone—the pain of betrayal, rejection, humiliation, and injustice—would be enough to kill any man. I believe Christ agonized over those things in the Garden of Gethsemane. The suffering of His soul over those things almost killed Him, prompting His body to sweat great drops of blood (Luke 22:44). The nails in His hands were nothing compared to the pain of bearing all the sins of all the people who ever lived, or the pain of enduring undeserved humiliation and rejection.

B. Physical Suffering

1. Injury

Scourging was a horrible thing. Forty lashes were given by both the Jews and the Romans. The Jews always stopped one short of forty because they didn't want to break the law (2 Cor. 11:24; cf. Deut. 25:3). The Jews gave thirteen lashes across the chest, and then thirteen on each shoulder. It usually took two men to do it because one wasn't strong enough to continue the whipping at the desired pace. The victim's hands were tied to a post, making the body taut. When the scourging was complete the organs would be exposed. The bleeding was often so profuse that many would die. Jesus suffered a tremendous amount of physical pain before He ever reached the cross.

2. Death

How did Jesus die? I don't think He died from the nails in His hands. I don't think the crown of thorns killed Him. It is possible that the suffocation of His organs is the physiological reason for His death. But I think He died from cumulative grief, anxiety, pain, and suffering.

The greatest suffering is not physical; it is the suffering of the soul. Isaiah, through the inspiration of the Holy Spirit, gives us some understanding of the degree of Christ's suffering. That's what Christ tried to tell the disciples, but they didn't come close to understanding because the next thing you read is about James and John's attempt to reserve seats in the kingdom next to Christ. They were completely insensitive. So you might add one other thing that Jesus suffered: the pain of unsympathetic friends. He experienced the suffering that comes when you need people but find they're unresponsive to your needs because they are so involved in seeking their own glory.

IV. THE POWER OF HIS SUFFERINGS

Matthew 20:19 says, "The third day he shall rise again." Suffering was not Jesus' end. People who say that Jesus' revolution ended in a grave are wrong. He rose out of that grave three days later. Psalm 16:10 says, "Thou wilt not leave my soul in sheol, neither wilt thou permit thine Holy One to see corruption." Jesus burst out of that grave and is alive to this very day. That is the power He had over His sufferings. He said He would conquer death. How could the disciples miss that part of His teaching? Why didn't they pursue the matter?

V. THE PERCEPTION OF HIS SUFFERINGS

Matthew 20:20-22 says, "Then came to him the mother of Zebedee's children with her sons, worshiping him, and desiring a certain thing of him. And he said unto her, What wilt thou? She saith unto him, Grant that these, my two sons, may sit, the one on thy right hand, and the other on the left, in thy kingdom. But Jesus answered and said, Ye know not what ye ask." They didn't ask Jesus to explain His suffering to them. They didn't ask Him to tell them more about redemption, about the ransom, or about His resurrection. They just asked Him if they could sit on His right and left when the kingdom came. They didn't get the message. They wanted a King, but they didn't understand that they needed a Savior first.

The disciples are no different than many people today. They don't mind Jesus as a little baby in a manger at Christmas. They don't mind Him when little children sit in His lap. They don't even mind Him too much as a King. But they can't handle Him as Savior. That is the case with Israel today. They won't accept the Messiah's need to suffer.

The good news has some bad news in it—there is a Savior, but He had to suffer. First Peter 3:18 says, "Christ also hath once suffered for sins, the just for the unjust, that he might bring us to God." We couldn't get there any other way. Why? When Adam and Eve sinned, they were separated from God. What reconciled them? A sacrifice. When God ordained the elaborate sacrificial system for Israel He was communicating that no one can come to Him unless it's by means of a sacrifice. Jesus had to be offered for sin as the ultimate sacrifice so that He might bring us to God for good.

Fortunately, the Holy Spirit came to the disciples on the Day of Pentecost. It was then that Peter was able to preach a tremendous sermon on the meaning of the death and resurrection of Christ. I'm glad they finally got the message. I hope you do too.

Focusing on the Facts

1. What is the center of biblical revelation (see p. 74)?
2. What is the theme of Matthew 20:17-19 (see pp. 74-75)?
3. What was Christ's attitude as He headed toward Jerusalem (Luke 9:51; see p. 76)?
4. Why were the disciples amazed and afraid about going to Jerusalem (Mark 10:32; see p. 77)?
5. What kind of amazement did the disciples experience? (see p. 78)?
6. What are some of the Old Testament prophecies that Jesus fulfilled (see p. 79)?
7. What had to happen before God could clothe Adam and Eve? What does that teach about how sin and guilt were to be dealt with (see p. 80)?
8. What sustained Abraham in his faith in God's promise when it looked like he would kill the fulfillment of it (Heb. 11:19; see p. 80)?
9. What truth of redemption is established in God's provision of a ram for the sacrifice (Gen. 22:10-13; see p. 81)?
10. What redemptive truth can be learned from the institution of the Passover (Ex. 12:3-5; see p. 81)?
11. What ended when Christ died on the cross and the veil of the Temple was ripped in half (Matt. 27:51; see p. 82)?
12. How was Christ able to know about all the things that were going to happen to Him (see p. 83)?
13. Who were the chief priests? Who were the scribes (see p. 84)?
14. Why did the chief priests and scribes condemn Jesus to death (see p. 85)?
15. Why did they have to turn Jesus over to the Romans (see p. 85)?
16. Describe what happened to Jesus when He was brought to Fort Antonia (see p. 85).
17. Why did the executioners often scourge their victims before crucifying them (see p. 86)?

18. In what ways does Isaiah 53 reveal the proportion of Christ's suffering (see pp. 86-87)?
19. In what ways did Jesus suffer the pain of disloyalty (see p. 88)?
20. In what ways did Jesus suffer the pain of rejection (see p. 88)?
21. What was the injustice that Christ had to endure (see p. 89)?
22. What is the power of Christ's sufferings (Matt. 20:19; see p. 90)?

Pondering the Principles

1. Although the need to make continual sacrifice for sin ended when Jesus became the final sacrifice, we are still not absolved from making sacrifices to God. Read Hebrews 13:15-16. What two types of sacrifices does the writer of Hebrews refer to? How often have you made either type of sacrifice over the past week? God is well pleased when you offer them, so make the commitment to do so this week. To help in this, read Psalm 145:1-11 and memorize 1 John 3:18.

2. Read Isaiah 53. Next, write out the entire chapter. As you write, change the our's and we's to my's, I's, and me's. Then read what you have written. That is what your Savior did for you. He is not someone else's Savior; He is yours. Talk to Jesus Christ right now and thank Him for the intimacy you have in your relationship with Him. As you pray, remember all that He suffered for you. Ask the Lord to continually remind you of that every day, especially on those days when He asks you to suffer for Him.

5
How to Be Great in the Kingdom—Part 1

Outline

Introduction
A. The Celebration of Pride
   1. In the world
   2. In the church
B. The Confrontation of Scripture
   1. The denunciation of pride
     a) The definitions of pride
     b) The downfall of pride
   2. The exaltation of humility
     a) Micah 6:8
     b) Psalm 138:6
     c) Psalm 10:17
     d) Proverbs 15:33
C. The Correction of Christ
   1. Regarding glory
   2. Regarding suffering
     a) The sufferings of Christ
     b) The sufferings of the disciples
       (1) Expect nothing from the world
       (2) Expect to die
   3. Regarding humility
     a) The lesson of self-denial
     b) The lie of self-glory
       (1) Believed by the disciples
       (2) Believed by Christians

Lesson
I. How Not to Be Great (vv. 20-25)
A. Political Power Play (vv. 20-21)

1. The proponents of the power play (v. 20)
2. The proposition of the power play (v. 21)
   a) An advantageous relationship
   b) A manipulative reverence
   c) A sinful request
      (1) The motivation of the mother
      (2) The motivation of James and John
B. Audacious Ambition (vv. 22-24)
   1. The ignorance of James and John (v. 22a)
   2. The implications of the request (vv. 22b-23a)
      a) Exalted commitment (v. 22b)
      b) Excessive confidence (v. 22c)
      c) Eventual commission (v. 23a)
   3. The inclination of God (v. 23b)
   4. The indignation of the ten (v. 24)
C. Dominant Dictatorship (v. 25a)
   1. In the world
   2. In the church
D. Charismatic Control (v. 25b)
Conclusion

Introduction

A. The Celebration of Pride

1. In the world

We live in a proud and egotistical generation. People continually promote themselves. I can't remember a time when there was more acceptance and promotion of pride as a virtue. During the time of the Roman Empire, pride was exalted as a virtue, and humility was viewed as a weakness. I used to wonder how a society could reach that point. But now I see the same thing occurring in our society. It may well mark the demise of our society, just as it did Roman society. No society can survive when pride runs rampant.

Society depends on meaningful, ongoing, and supportive relationships. But when a mass of people are committed to themselves alone, relationships will disintegrate. And that is exactly what is happening in our society—relationships are falling apart. Everyone is consumed with his own rights—with self-glory, self-esteem, self-promotion, and pride. People parade their pride as if it were a virtue. Even the business world is based on pride and self-promotion.

2. In the church

Sadly, that tendency has found its way into Christianity. People are now twisting the Bible to promote pride and self-esteem. There are so-called Christian books on how to make your body and face more beautiful. I even saw one that told how to buy a wardrobe that matched your skin color. Those are not spiritual issues.

Since the early 70s we have seen the cult of selfism burgeon in the church of Jesus Christ. We live in a Christian age that now believes God's only design for us is to be healthy, wealthy, happy, satisfied, and fulfilled. We know little about sacrifice or the pain of suffering. Many want to eliminate that part of Christianity. Most of us are consumed with creature comforts and travel in our quest to fulfill what we believe to be deep needs. In the process, we have begun to exalt pride and forget humility. There was a time in the church when many preached about humility. During the time of the Reformation and the Puritans, there was a sense of brokenness and contrition in the church. People trembled at the Word of God. The humility and meekness that existed within the church gave it great power. But today the church wants to be proud, fulfilled, and indulgent. It has fallen prey to the sin of pride. It has replaced humility as a virtue, and humility has been labeled as a weakness.

B. The Confrontation of Scripture

1. The denunciation of pride

The Bible is clear about the sin of pride.

a) The definitions of pride

    (1) Proverbs 21:4—"A proud heart . . . [is] sin."

    (2) Proverbs 16:5—"Every one who is proud in heart is an abomination to the Lord."

    (3) Proverbs 8:13—"The fear of the Lord is to hate evil; pride, and arrogance."

    (4) Romans 1:30—Pride is a mark of the reprobate mind.

    (5) 1 Timothy 3:6—Pride comes from the devil.

    (6) 1 John 2:16—Pride is a part of the world.

    (7) 1 Timothy 6:3-4—Pride is characteristic of false teachers.

b) The downfall of pride

    (1) James 4:6—"God resisteth the proud."

    (2) Isaiah 23:9—God brings the proud into contempt.

    (3) Psalm 31:23—The proud will be judged.

    (4) Exodus 18:11—The proud will be subdued.

    (5) Psalm 18:27—The proud will be brought low.

    (6) Daniel 4:37—The proud will be abased.

    (7) Luke 1:51—The proud will be scattered.

    (8) Malachi 4:1—The proud will be punished.

2. The exaltation of humility

Humility is exalted as a virtue in the Bible. We need to understand that in terms of our experience as well.

a) Micah 6:8—"What doth the Lord require of thee, but to do justly, and to love mercy, and to walk humbly with thy God?"

b) Psalm 138:6—"Though the Lord be high, yet hath he respect unto the lowly."

c) Psalm 10:17—"Lord, Thou hast heard the desire of the humble."

d) Proverbs 15:33—"Before honor is humility."

The Lord lifts up the humble (James 4:10). Colossians 3:12 instructs us to put on humility. First Peter 5:5 tells us to be clothed with humility. And Ephesians 4:1-2 says we are to walk in humility. If you desire honor and glory from God, you must display humility first. That is contrary to our earthly philosophy, which exalts pride.

C. The Correction of Christ

We need to learn that honor comes through humility and that glory comes through suffering. The disciples sought the high places in God's kingdom. The Lord needed to correct that attitude, and He confronts it in Matthew 20:20-28. Unfortunately He was forced to teach the same lesson a few days later.

1. Regarding glory

The disciples basically forsook all to follow Jesus. They followed Him out of genuine love and admiration, yet they also knew that whatever they gave up would be more than replenished when He entered into His kingdom, for Jesus said, "In the regeneration, when the Son of man shall sit on the throne of his glory, ye also shall sit upon twelve thrones, judging the twelve tribes of Israel. And every one that hath forsaken houses, or brethren, or sisters, or father, or mother, or wife, or children, or lands, for my name's sake, shall receive an hundredfold, and shall inherit everlasting life" (Matt. 19:28-29). Those are some powerful promises. Unfortunately, it fed their materialistic thinking, even

99

though it wasn't intended to. When Jesus talked about suffering, they didn't understand because they didn't listen. They were too interested in what He said about glory, honor, and reigning in the kingdom.

2. Regarding suffering

   a) The sufferings of Christ

   In Matthew 20:17-19, Jesus gives for a third time a description of what His death would be like. His previous discussions are presented in Matthew 16:21 and 17:22-23. He told His disciples that He was going to Jerusalem to suffer and to die. He was trying to balance their perspective. There is going to be a kingdom, but the way to it is through suffering. First comes death, then glory. Humility is before honor (Prov. 15:33).

   b) The sufferings of the disciples

   Jesus also taught the disciples about their own suffering.

   (1) Expect nothing from the world

   In Matthew 8:20 Jesus tells a would-be disciple that before he followed Him he ought to know, "The foxes have holes, and the birds of the air have nests, but the Son of man hath not where to lay His head." In other words, "If you follow Me, I can't promise you a thing—not even a place to sleep."

   (2) Expect to die

   Jesus said He had come to bring a sword and to set a person against his own family (Matt. 10:34-39). In Matthew 16:24 He says, "If any man will come after me, let him deny himself, and take up his cross, and follow me." That meant death.

The disciples received many lessons about suffering—about their own and Christ's—but it never seemed to sink in because they were so intent on learning about their glory and greatness in the kingdom.

3. Regarding humility

   a) The lesson of self-denial

   Jesus emphasizes humility in Matthew 18:3-4 when He says that anyone who would come into His kingdom must humble himself as a little child. They needed to learn to deny themselves. That's a mark of a true follower of Jesus Christ. He tried to get the same message across to the rich young ruler when he said, "If thou wilt be perfect, go and sell what thou hast, and give to the poor, and thou shalt have treasures in heaven; and come and follow me" (Matt. 19:21). But the man wouldn't do it. That was a profound lesson about the requirements for entering into the kingdom—humility, self-denial, and abandonment.

   b) The lie of self-glory

   (1) Believed by the disciples

   The disciples could have forsaken all and followed Jesus without ever asking what was in it for them, but they didn't. In Matthew 19:27 Peter asks, "What shall we have, therefore?" The human heart is treacherous. Selfishness is incurable in this life; it only can be brought under control. They should have understood their service to Christ as a service of love without thought of receiving anything in return. The humble person seeks no glory, no esteem, no honor, no promotion, and no popularity. In Matthew 20:17-19 Jesus talks about His suffering and death, but all the disciples could think about was their own self-glory.

After Jesus taught the disciples about humility, they soon proved they didn't get the message. In the upper room the night Judas betrayed Christ, the disciples continued to argue about who would be the greatest in the kingdom. The Lord was again telling them of His own death, and they were still debating about which of them was going to sit in the chief seats in the kingdom.

(2) Believed by Christians

The same thing is true today. Jesus is still saying, "Take up your cross." Humility is still the path to glory. He still wants us to abandon ourselves to ministry. We should be willing to give up everything we have in this world to do what Christ wants no matter what the cost. But people are still missing that lesson. They see grace merely as a free ticket to the storehouse of divine goodies—that all God wants to do is make you healthy, wealthy, and happy.

I trust none of you are approaching the Christian life for what it can give you. God has not called us to that; He's called us to humility. He's called us to suffer. Second Timothy 2:12 says, "If we suffer, we shall also reign with Him." First Peter 5:10 says, "After ye have suffered awhile, [God will] make you perfect." Romans 8:18 says, "The sufferings of this present time are not worthy to be compared with the glory which shall be revealed in us." As we suffer here, we're glorified in heaven. If we seek glory here, we forfeit it there (Matt. 16:25).

Voices of Reason

Paul Brownback has written a helpful book entitled *The Danger of Self Love* (Chicago: Moody, 1982). In it he says, "Almost immediately the Christian public felt warmly at home with its newfound friend; self-love has been easily incorporated into the mind-set of evangelical Christians. All one needs to do to verify this is to walk into his Sunday school class next Sunday morning and ask, 'Should a Christian love himself?' He probably will discover quickly that the tide of opinion flows strongly toward a positive response" (p. 13). That is not biblical Christianity. Neither is it historic Christianity. Brownback cites the following:

1. John Piper—"Today the first and greatest commandment is, 'Thou shalt love thyself.' And the explanation for almost every interpersonal problem is thought to lie in someone's low self-esteem. Sermons, articles, and books have pushed this idea into the Christian mind. It is a rare congregation, for example, that does not stumble over the 'vermicular theology' of Isaac Watts's 'Alas! And Did My Savior Bleed': 'Would He devote that sacred head/For such a worm as I?' " ("Is Self-Love Biblical?" *Christianity Today*, 12 August 1977, p. 6). People don't like that. One of the letters written to the editor at *Moody Monthly* in response to an article I wrote on Robert Schuller's book *Self Esteem* said, "MacArthur has become a victim of worm theology." Humility is not a popular theme in a day when men promote themselves.

2. John Stott—"A chorus of many voices is chanting in unison today that I must at all costs love myself" ("Must I Really Love Myself?" *Christianity Today*, 5 May 1978, p. 34).

3. Saint Augustine—"Two cities have been formed by two loves; the earthly by the love of self, even to the contempt of God, the heavenly by the love of God even to the contempt of self. The former, in a word, glories in itself, the latter in the Lord" (*The City of God* XIV.28).

4. John Calvin—"For so blindly do we all rush in the direction of self-love that everyone thinks he has a good reason for exalting himself and despising all others in comparison." Calvin offers a cure for the problem: "There is no other remedy than to pluck up by the roots those most noxious pests, self-love and love of victory. . . . This the doctrine of Scripture does. For it teaches us to remember, that the endowments which God has bestowed upon us are not our own, but His free gifts, and that those who plume themselves upon them betray their ingratitude" (*Institutes of the Christian Religion*, trans. Henry Beveridge [Grand Rapids: Eerdmans, 1966]: 2:10).

The historical leaders of the church confronted the problem of self-love, and we are facing the same problem today. There's a magazine available now called *Self*, which leaves little doubt regarding its content. Some people have gone so far as to change the words in some of the hymns, removing lines such as "mine own worthlessness," or "my sinful self, my only shame."

We need to reexamine the idea of humility as a path to glory. And that is precisely what we will do in Matthew 20:20-28. I want to examine two points: how not to be great and how to be great.

Lesson

I. HOW NOT TO BE GREAT (vv. 20-25)

Four worldly ways to seek greatness are given in verses 20-25: two by example and two by instruction of our Lord. Men pursue greatness through earthly means, but such ways are not adaptable to God's kingdom. Jesus said, "My kingdom is not of this world" (John 18:36).

A. Political Power Play (vv. 20-21)

The world tells us that if you want to get something or somewhere, it all depends on who you know. If you want to climb the ladder of success, you're told to get next to the people who have the influence. Political power play is a common approach to reach places of prominence and glory in this world. You can manipulate people and circumstances to get close to those who can pull you to the top. One pastor commented some years ago that whenever he attended his denomination's convention, he always tried to get a hotel room next to the men in charge so he could get to know them. That way he would be assured of getting bigger and bigger churches.

1. The proponents of the power play (v. 20)

"Then came to him the mother of Zebedee's children with her sons [James and John], worshiping him, and desiring a certain thing of him."

104

It amazes me that this event happened right on the heels of Jesus' explanation of His coming death (Matt. 20:17-19). James, John, and their mother seem to be completely indifferent to that. (In fact, no mention is made that any of the disciples even responded to what Jesus said.) Mark 10:35-41 is a comparative passage, but there the mother is not even mentioned. It's important that we don't think she was on her own or that they were just tagging along. They came as a trio.

2. The proposition of the power play (v. 21)

"And he said unto her, What wilt thou? She saith unto him, Grant that these, my two sons, may sit, the one on thy right hand, and the other on the left, in thy kingdom."

That was an act of pride. James and John wanted the chief places in the kingdom. They were seeking self-glory, honor, and esteem. They wanted to sit next to Christ so people could say, "Look at how close they are to Christ. They must be the second and third most holy people." They sought affirmation from people.

Both James and John were bold. If you don't think so, then read Mark 9:38 and Luke 9:54. They were called "Sons of thunder" (Mark 3:17). We often think of them as passive because Jesus spoke of John so endearingly. But they both were brash, bold, and demanding men who were trying to make a political power play on Jesus.

a) An advantageous relationship

Matthew, Mark, and John tell us that when Jesus was being crucified, some women stood at the foot of the cross. Matthew 27:56 gives their names as: Mary Magdalene, Mary, the mother of James and Joseph, and the mother of the sons of Zebedee. Mark 15:40 says they were Mary Magdalene, Mary the mother of James and Joses, and Salome (who must then be the mother of the sons of Zebedee). John 19:25 says, "There stood by the cross of Jesus his mother, and his mother's sister, Mary, the wife of

Clopas, and Mary Magdalene." We know who Mary Magdalene is. We know who Jesus' mother is. Mary, the wife of Clopas must be the mother of James and Joseph. That leaves the other woman— Salome, the mother of the sons of Zebedee—who is now called Jesus' mother's sister. Therefore, the mother of the sons of Zebedee is the sister of Mary, the mother of Jesus.

Do you understand the politics? Advancement is seen as a matter of who you know. James and John wanted to play on the affection of Jesus for His mother. So they used their ace in the hole: they were Jesus' cousins—their mothers were sisters. And they didn't come just as cousins: they brought their mother along to play on Jesus' sympathy for His aunt.

b) A manipulative reverence

Jesus' aunt worshiped (Gk., *proskuneō*) Him. She bowed down and treated Him like a king. Verse 20 says she was "desiring a certain thing of him." She wouldn't tell Him what she desired (Mark 10:35). She wanted Him to promise to give it to her before she told Him what it was. Now that is childish. Have you ever had your child do that to you? Standard procedure in our home is never to say yes to things we don't know about. I think the mother's approach betrayed some doubt in her heart about the legitimacy of her request. It also betrayed great ambition on the part of James and John. They wanted the seats so badly that they were willing to corner Christ into promising something they believed He wouldn't do if He knew what it was.

The approach James, John, and their mother used was a common method of exalting a king. For example, Herod Antipas told Salome, after her dancing, that he would give her anything she wanted (Matt. 14:7). In that way a king showed how far-reaching his power was. So the mother treated Jesus like a king. She thought she could appeal to Him on the basis of His love of royalty and power. It was an extremely manipulative approach.

c) A sinful request

    (1) The motivation of the mother

She did not ask Jesus for herself; she would receive her glory through the honor given to her two sons. There is some virtue in her desire: she revealed that she believed Christ would bring about His kingdom. But apart from that, there's no virtue in the request at all. It is sinful because it seeks glory for James and John. Suppose you and your mother go to Jesus and she says, "Of all the people who have ever served God, I believe my sons ought to sit on your right and left hand in the kingdom." You would no doubt feel awkward in using such a brash approach.

    (2) The motivation of James and John

You might be wondering how James and John could conceive of making such a request. For one thing, they were Jesus' cousins. In that sense they had a certain intimacy with Him. They were also in the inner-circle of the disciples, which included Peter. They knew Peter was continually being rebuked by Christ, so they probably thought he couldn't qualify for a chief seat. They weren't any better than Peter, but they had learned to keep their thoughts to themselves, so they appeared to be more holy. Based on their relationship to Christ and Peter's disqualification, they figured it was a legitimate request. Why did they want to sit to the right and left of Christ? Because they wanted to be glorified.

The church still suffers from people who seek preeminence. They are like the Pharisees, who loved the chief seats in the synagogues, wanting to sit above men and be called Father (Matt. 23:

6-9). There are always people in the church who want to be esteemed and lifted up, thinking that they will receive an eternal reward as a result. But our Lord rejects political power play. That is not how you reach a place of blessing and honor in the kingdom.

B. Audacious Ambition (vv. 22-24)

1. The ignorance of James and John (v. 22*a*)

"But Jesus answered and said, Ye know not what ye ask."

They were asking for glory but didn't realize that the path to glory is suffering. The highest places of glory are reserved for those who endure the greatest degree of suffering. From time to time I'm asked, "Who will receive the greatest reward in heaven?" The answer is given in the Word of God: those who suffered the most in this life for the cause of Jesus Christ—those who confronted a hostile world and paid the greatest price in self-denial for His purposes.

Second Corinthians 4:17 says, "Our light affliction, which is but for a moment, worketh for us a far more exceeding and eternal weight of glory." What leads to glory? Affliction. Now that does not refer to physical affliction from illness or affliction associated with carelessness or sin. But when we are persecuted for the cause of the gospel, we are building up a greater inheritance of glory in eternity. As we learned in Matthew 20:1-16, we all equally receive eternal life. Similarly we all inherit the perfection of Christ's likeness in eternity, yet there is a greater weight of glory reserved for those who suffered the most for the cause of Christ in this life.

2. The implications of the request (vv. 22*b*-23*a*)

a) Exalted commitment (v. 22*b*)

"Are you able to drink of the cup that I shall drink of?"

Jesus was going to be exalted as a result of His suffering. If James and John wanted to sit beside Him in the kingdom, then they needed to be willing to seek the same degree of suffering that He would experience.

The word *cup* is used as an Old Testament symbol that meant "to take everything in." Our Lord is saying, "Are you able to suffer to the degree that I will?" Its use is reminiscent of Isaiah 51:17, 22, which refers to the cup of God's fury. Christ drank of that cup to the last. So He asks the disciples if they are able to do likewise.

Christ was exalted to full glory because He endured such profound suffering. Because He suffered the most; He is glorified the most. Whoever suffers most next to Him will be glorified next to Him. Our eternal weight of glory is predicated on suffering. If you seek such glory, you will achieve it only through humility, suffering, and self-sacrifice—not by political power play or audacious ambition.

b) Excessive confidence (v. 22c)

"They say unto him, We are able."

They weren't able. They had audacious ambition. Many people plunge into a task believing they can do it. This old adage remains true: "They said it couldn't be done, but he hopped right to it and couldn't do it." That's often true in the spiritual dimension. I believe some of us have excessive confidence. If you believe you can do something in your own strength, you can't.

Peter told Christ, "Though all men shall be offended because of thee, yet will I never be offended" (Matt. 26:33). Yet before a cock crowed, he denied the Lord three times. James, John, and all the rest of the disciples fled when Jesus was taken prisoner (Matt. 26:56). They couldn't handle the danger. James and John may have thought they were able, but they obviously weren't. They were plagued by their audacious ambition. You can't move your way up the kingdom's ladder of honor and glory by boasting in your self-confidence. Neither can you climb it by a manipulative political power play.

c) Eventual commission (v. 23*a*)

"And he saith unto them, Ye shall drink indeed of my cup."

The disciples would taste of Christ's cup of suffering, but they would never drink the whole thing. The time came when they were faithful. We know James was faithful because he was the first apostle to be martyred (Acts 12:2). John was faithful, for he was exiled to the Isle of Patmos for the rest of his life on account of Christ. They did drink of the cup. They experienced the fellowship of His sufferings, if not the fullness of them. But they were not able to drink of the cup until the Spirit came and infused them with internal spiritual strength.

3. The inclination of God (v. 23*b*)

"But to sit on my right hand, and on my left, is not mine to give, but it shall be given to them for whom it is prepared by my Father."

Christ was in submission to the Father. Only God can pass out the rewards. He ultimately gives glory to whomever He wills. I've often wondered who will be the greatest in heaven. The only possible answer is the one who suffered the most to proclaim the name of Jesus Christ. It certainly won't be anyone who has sought glory by political power play or audacious ambition. It is prepared for those who have been smitten with "worm theology" and have lived it out.

4. The indignation of the ten (v. 24)

"And when the ten heard it, they were moved with indignation against the two brethren."

The other ten disciples weren't being spiritual; they were angry because James and John asked for the chief seats before they did. Luke 22:24-27 tells us that days later they were all arguing about who would be greatest in the kingdom.

C. Dominant Dictatorship (v. 25a)

"Jesus called them unto him, and said, Ye know that the princes of the Gentiles exercise dominion over them."

The Greek word translated "exercise dominion over" is *katakurieuō*, which means "to lord it over." Another way people of the world seek greatness is through dominant dictatorship.

1. In the world

The Caesars, the Ptolemys of Egypt, the Herods, Antiochus Epiphanes, Pilate, Hitler, Idi Amin, and the Shah of Iran were all dictators. They ruled by lording their authority over people. One of the reasons Africa is so susceptible to communist revolution and the reason for unending rebellion in Latin and Central America is that those nations are coming out of dominant dictatorships. Many of the leaders in those countries filled their coffers at the expense of the people. In reaction to that, the people became fertile soil for communist infiltration, resulting in the kind of chaos that leads to Communism.

2. In the church

Leadership in some churches is dictatorial. Certain leaders dominate everyone in the church by telling them what to believe and how to act. There are those leaders, like Jim Jones, whose strange movements have moved closer to mainstream Christianity than his ever did. I've heard more times than I'd like to remember from people who have said they can't tell their pastor anything. Peter specifically told pastors not to lord their authority over the people (1 Pet. 5:3).

D. Charismatic Control (v. 25*b*)

"They that are great [Gk., *megalos*, "the chief ones"] exercise authority over them."

The Greek word translated "exercise authority" is *katexousiazō*, which means "to vaunt power." Colloquially it means "to throw your weight around." It seems best to see this as the power of personality. Dominant dictatorship is the power of position; charismatic control is the power of personality. This type of leader has the charm, charisma, wit, and glibness that give him power in swaying people. There are many people who achieve greatness in the world by virtue of their charismatic personality.

Such people also exist within the church. You might have asked yourself how people are able to listen to certain preachers and teachers and believe what they say. They certainly aren't intimidated by them, but they are enamored by their personality. Those kinds of preachers and teachers know what psychological tricks and gimmicks will move people to fall prey to their leadership.

We received a series of correspondence from a woman who was under a dominant dictatorship in her church. The pastor wanted to totally control her life. It nearly drove her to suicide. That shows the tremendous power a dominant dictatorship can have. We counseled her, and fortunately the Lord has delivered her. We have also received letters from people who have been delivered out of the control of leaders who had subtle ways of convincing them that they were of God.

Conclusion

Our Lord tells us not to seek greatness by a political power play. Don't try to climb the ladder of success based on who you know. Don't seek it by audacious ambition; don't overstate your abilities. Don't seek it by dominant dictatorship; don't try to pull rank on people. And don't use your personality to manipulate others. If you want to be great, learn the lesson that Jesus teaches in

Matthew 20:22. Before honor comes humility. Before you can wear the crown, you have to drink the cup. The way to exaltation is the way of humility. Seek to know God and walk humbly with Him. Matthew 20:26-28 gives us the way to greatness in the kingdom: "It shall not be so among you, but whosoever will be great among you, let him be your minister, and whosoever will be chief among you, let him be your servant; even as the Son of man came not to be ministered unto, but to minister, and to give his life a ransom for many."

Focusing on the Facts

1. Why have relationships within our society reached a stress point (see pp. 96-97)?
2. In what way has the church begun to follow the example of the world (see p. 97)?
3. What marked the churches in the Reformation and Puritan eras (see p. 97)?
4. Define pride (see pp. 97-98).
5. What must a Christian display before he can ever receive glory and honor from God (see p. 99)?
6. What did Jesus teach the disciples about their own suffering (see p. 100)?
7. How do we know that the disciples did not learn from Jesus' teaching about suffering in Matthew 20:17-19 (see pp. 101-2)?
8. Define the strategy of political power play (see p. 104).
9. What special relationship did James, John, and their mother have with Jesus (see pp. 105-6)?
10. What motivated the mother of James and John to do what she did (see p. 106)?
11. What motivated James and John to do what they did (see p. 106)?
12. For whom are the highest places in glory reserved (see p. 108)?
13. What leads to glory (see p. 108)?
14. What was the cup Jesus referred to in Matthew 20:22 (see p. 108)?
15. Both James and John said they were able to drink of the cup, but they fled when the time came (Matt. 26:56). What finally gave them the ability to drink from the cup (see p. 109)?
16. Why did the other ten disciples become indignant with James and John (see p. 110)?

17. Describe the strategy of dominant dictatorship (see pp. 110-11).
18. Describe the strategy of charismatic control (see pp. 111-12).

Pondering the Principles

1. Proverbs 15:33 says, "Before honor is humility." How often do you get the order of the two mixed up? Read James 4:1-10. What happens when you exalt yourself? What happens when you humble yourself before God? Remember, "friendship with the world is hostility toward God" (v. 4, NASB*). In this past week, have you shown any hostility toward God? The world is characterized by pride. Make it your goal this week to begin rooting out pride in your life and developing a humble attitude.

2. Review the four ways not to be great in God's kingdom (see pp. 104-12). Give examples of your behavior that have revealed tendencies to gain greatness through each of those ways. How can you specifically apply Matthew 20:26-27 to each of those areas? Be diligent in your application.

*New American Standard Bible.

6

How to Be Great in the Kingdom—Part 2

Outline

Introduction
A. Great Men of the Old Testament
B. Great Men of the New Testament

Review
I. How Not to Be Great (vv. 20-25)

Lesson
II. How to Be Great (vv. 26-28)
A. The Exhortation (vv. 26-27)
   1. The premise of greatness (v. 26a)
   2. The passion for greatness (v. 26b)
      a) The advocates of greatness
         (1) Jesus
         (2) Paul
         (3) John
      b) The attitude of sacrifice
         (1) A pure motive
         (2) A good desire
   3. The path of greatness (v. 26c-27)
      a) Service (v. 26c)
         (1) Demonstrated
         (2) Defined
         (3) Delineated
            (a) The commitment
            (b) The contrast
      b) Slavery (v. 27)
         (1) Affirming the path of pain
         (2) Avoiding the path of pain

B. The Example (v. 28)
1. The service of Christ (v. 28*a*)
   a) His humiliation
   b) His humanity
2. The death of Christ (v. 28*b-c*)
   a) The ultimate service (v. 28*b*)
   b) The ultimate ransom (v. 28*c*)
      (1) Its price
      (2) Its purpose
      (3) Its participants

Conclusion

Introduction

The lives of great men and women in God's kingdom are marked by humble service. They never seek to be lifted up to a prominent place. They serve God sacrificially with a heart of humility.

A. Great Men of the Old Testament

1. Abraham, a special servant of God, said, "Behold now, I have taken upon me to speak unto the Lord, who am but dust and ashes" (Gen. 18:27).

2. Isaac was willing to die as an offering to the Lord if that was what God required (Gen. 22:8-9).

3. Jacob cried out to God, "I am not worthy of the least of all the mercies, and of all the truth, which thou hast shown unto thy servant" (Gen. 32:10).

4. Joseph was dishonored and sold into slavery by his own brothers, yet he humbly forgave them and never retained any bitterness or vengeance in his heart. When he saw his brothers he wept, and then "comforted them, and spoke kindly unto them" (Gen. 50:17, 21).

5. Moses said to God, "Who am I, that I should go unto Pharaoh, and that I should bring forth the children of Israel out of Egypt?" (Ex. 3:11).

116

6. Joshua, when he faced the Lord after a defeat that came as a result of the Israelites' lack of faith, "tore his clothes, and fell to the earth upon his face before the ark of the Lord until the eventide, he and the elders of Israel, and put dust upon their heads" (Josh. 7:6).

7. Gideon, when called to lead his people, said, "O my Lord, wherewith shall I save Israel? Behold, my family is poor in Manasseh, and I am the least in my father's house" (Judg. 6:15).

8. David knew his own frailty and said the following in 1 Chronicles 29:10-16, one of the great humbling texts of all the Old Testament, "Praise be to you, O Lord, God of our father Israel, from everlasting to everlasting. Yours, O Lord, is the greatness and the power and the glory and the majesty and the splendor, for everything in heaven and earth is yours. Yours, O Lord, is the kingdom; you are exalted as head over all. Wealth and honor come from you; you are the ruler of all things. In your hands are strength and power to exalt and give strength to all. Now, our God, we give you thanks, and praise your glorious name. But who am I, and who are my people, that we should be able to give as generously as this? Everything comes from you, and we have given you only what comes from your hand. We are aliens and strangers in your sight, as were all our forefathers. Our days on earth are like a shadow, without hope. O Lord our God, as for all this abundance that we have provided for building you a temple for your Holy Name, it comes from your hand, and all of it belongs to you" (NIV).*

9. Hezekiah, the king of Judah, "humbled himself for the pride of his heart" (2 Chron. 32:26).

10. Manasseh, another king of Judah, "humbled himself greatly before the God of his fathers" (2 Chron. 33:12).

11. Josiah, king of Judah, was told this: "Because thine heart was tender, and thou didst humble thyself be-

New International Version.

fore God . . . and didst tear thy clothes, and [wept] before me, I have even heard thee also" (2 Chron. 34:27).

12. Job was humbled and repented in dust and ashes (Job 42:6).

13. Isaiah was so humbled that he cursed himself and cried out, "I am a man of unclean lips, and I dwell in the midst of a people of unclean lips" (Isa. 6:5). It was that kind of humility God could use, so He called Isaiah to be a great prophet.

14. Jeremiah said, "Ah, Lord God! Behold, I cannot speak; for I am a child" (Jer. 1:6).

B. Great Men of the New Testament

1. John the Baptist felt unworthy to baptize Jesus Christ (Matt. 3:14). He said later on, "He must increase, but I must decrease" (John 3:30). He also said, "He it is who, coming after me, is preferred before me, whose shoe's latchet I am not worthy to loose" (John 1:27). Jesus said, "There hath not risen a greater than John the Baptist" (Matt. 11:11). I believe John the Baptist was the greatest because he was the most humble.

2. Peter expressed his humility when he said to Jesus, "Depart from me; for I am a sinful man, O Lord" (Luke 5:8).

3. Paul was described as "serving the Lord with all humility of mind" (Acts 20:19).

Having a slave's perspective ushers us into the greatness of the kingdom. Jesus said, "Whosoever . . . shall humble himself as [a] little child, the same is greatest in the kingdom of heaven" (Matt. 18:4). James, reiterating a great Old Testament truth in Proverbs 3:34, said, "God resisteth the proud, but giveth grace unto the humble" (James 4:6). Greatness in God's kingdom is reserved for those who are humble. The Father has prepared eternal glory and greatness to its highest degree for those who are humble. So if we desire to pursue greatness, we must pursue it on the path of humility and service.

I. HOW NOT TO BE GREAT (vv. 20-25); see pp. 104-12)

Lesson

II. HOW TO BE GREAT (vv. 26-28)

A. The Exhortation (vv. 26-27)

1. The premise of greatness (v. 26a)

"But it shall not be so among you."

In the world, people achieve greatness through the methods of political power play, audacious ambition, dominant dictatorship, and charismatic control. But Jesus informs the disciples that they were in a kingdom where those methods were reversed. In John 18:36 Jesus says, "My kingdom is not of this world." What did He mean by that? He meant that His kingdom doesn't operate on the same principles as the kingdoms of this world. In the world, greatness is illustrated by a pyramid—you get on top of the pile and control everyone underneath you. Lutheran commentator Lenski said, "The Gentile idea of greatness is inverted, turned upside down, the pyramid resting on its apex, the great man not sitting atop the lesser men, but the great man bearing the lesser men on his back" (*The Interpretation of St. Matthew's Gospel* [Minneapolis: Augsburg, 1943], p. 791).

We are not to seek greatness in the kingdom as the world seeks greatness. Sadly, there are many Christians like James and John and their mother who pursue the limelight of Christianity—who seek prestige and power. They eagerly provide for themselves the creature comforts that will minister most to their physical bodies and their psychological needs. They may be esteemed by some to be great, but in God's estimation they are not. When the true evaluation is made in the end, they will find themselves far down the line from those who are truly great, whose lives were marked by humble, sacrificial service.

2. The passion for greatness (v. 26b)

"Whosoever will be great among you."

This phrase in the Greek text literally says, "Whoever wishes among you to become great." Some people think Jesus is accommodating an ungodly ambition. Is it right to want to be great? Is it right to seek a reward? Is it right to want to be a leader?

a) The advocates of greatness

(1) Jesus

The best defense is that Jesus clearly advocates greatness in verse 26. He never promoted sinful ambition. Jesus dealt with the sinful ambition of James and John, but He affirmed that it isn't wrong to seek to be great; it is wrong to seek it for the wrong reason.

(2) Paul

Paul said, "Run in such a way that you may win" (1 Cor. 9:24, NASB). He also said we ought to be concerned that our works will stand the test of fire at the judgment seat of Christ. They should not be wood, hay, and stubble; but gold, silver, and precious stones (1 Cor. 3:12-13). Paul said, "We all must appear before the judgment seat of Christ, that everyone may receive the things done in his body, according to that he hath done, whether it be good or bad" (2 Cor. 5:10).

(3) John

The apostle John said, "Look to yourselves, that we lose not those things which we have wrought, but that we receive a full reward" (2

120

John 8). And at the climax of the Bible, we are told that the Lord said, "Behold, I come quickly, and my reward is with me, to give every man according as his work shall be" (Rev. 22:12).

It is not wrong to seek glory and exaltation in eternity. The Lord has given us that as a goal. But it is wrong to seek exaltation with a wrong motive, like James and John did. It is also wrong when you seek to lord it over others, be more esteemed than others in this life, or have greater authority, power, and comfort.

b) The attitude of sacrifice

To seek greatness in God's kingdom, you must be ready to suffer. Those are God's terms. God's path to glory is the path of sacrificial service. That means the path is self-effacing. There are those who seek glory but would avoid the pain. Yet there are those who seek glory through the pain, and it is they who seek on God's terms.

(1) A pure motive

Paul said, "With me it is a very small thing that I should be judged of you, or of man's judgment; yea, I judge not mine own self. For I know nothing against myself, yet I am not hereby justified; but he that judgeth me is the Lord. Therefore, judge nothing before the time, until the Lord come, who both will bring to light the hidden things of darkness, and will make manifest the counsels of the hearts; and then shall every man have praise of God" (1 Cor. 4:3-5). Only God can read our motives.

If a man seeks to give his life for Christ, if he seeks to be the best teacher or disciple he can be and willingly seeks it through the path of self-sacrifice, humility, and suffering, then he has a pure motive.

(2) A good desire

Paul said, "If a man desire the office of a bishop [overseer], he desireth a good work" (1 Tim. 3:1). I'm in the ministry today because I wanted to be. When I first came to Grace Church someone asked me, "How did you know you were called to the ministry?" I knew because it was my desire, and I believe God planted it in my heart. The only way you know you're called into ministry in the New Testament age is to have the desire. The church then looks at your life to see if you qualify to serve in that capacity.

It is the desire of my life to give everything I've got in service to Christ. I want to fulfill my spiritual gifts and maximize my potential. I don't want to forfeit any of it because of sin in my life.

3. The path of greatness (v. 26c-27)

a) Service (v. 26c)

"Let him be your servant."

(1) Demonstrated

The path of greatness is service. You don't want to get tied down to this world. Don't waste your time trying to pad your life with creature comforts and psychological affirmation. Too many people want to live a life of ease without having to deal with pressure and anxiety. Don't get caught in this culture's mad dash for leisure. People wear themselves out trying to relax! What you do need to do is abandon yourself for the purpose of the kingdom. Be a servant— that's what Christ is saying.

Grace Church receives many letters from people across the country who would like to come and serve on our staff. No doubt they would be a tremendous blessing from God and a great help to us. But we have an established principle from Scripture that you cannot lead until you have proven you can serve. We respond to those people by saying we appreciate their desire to lead but recommend that they come on their own and serve among us first. Should God approve of their service, He might be pleased to lift them up to a place of responsible leadership. Unfortunately that way of looking at things is foreign to most people. Nonetheless, I believe it is consistent with the Word of God. In the case of those who wish to come here, many of them have been approved in the place where they minister. It is hard for them to see the need to establish themselves in another place.

(2) Defined

The Greek word translated "servant" in verse 26 is *diakonos*. The word *deacon* comes from it. Many of us think "deacon" is a religious word, and in our society it is. But in the time of the New Testament, it was a secular word. It referred to low menial service. Someone would hire a deacon to clean up the yard, serve a meal, collect the garbage, or any other menial job. It's not a dishonoring term; it's merely an indicator of a low status in society. A deacon didn't need a lot of education, training, or skill; he just needed to be willing to serve.

The word *diakonos* is the word used most in the New Testament to speak of the service of Christians. It was not as though there were no other words the New Testament writers had to choose from. They could have used the word translated "priest," which is a somewhat exalted term. They could have used the term *archon*, which refers to a ruler or leader—one in a responsible position. They could have used *timē*—one in a place of honor. But the word chosen by the Spirit of God was *diakonos*. God is looking for those who come to serve.

(3) Delineated

(a) The commitment

In 1 Corinthians 4, the apostle Paul marks out his own attitude as a servant. He spoke of himself in a humble way. In verse 1 he calls himself a servant, only he uses the Greek word *hupēretēs,* which refers to a slave who pulled an oar while chained to a post in the hull of a great ship. Paul made the claim that he was a third-level galley slave, an under-rower for Christ. He had the right perspective. The Lord helped him have that humble perspective by leaving him with a thorn in the flesh (2 Cor. 12:7). He was also helped by God, who brought pain, anxiety, and suffering into his life. Paul's failures helped him have a humble perspective. Both Demas and John Mark (at least in the early years of his association with Paul) failed him in ministry. He had enough failure with his successes to know God was at work. Paul's humility helped him to rightly evaluate himself. In 1 Corinthians 3:5 he says, "Who, then, is Paul, and who is Apollos, but ministers [servants]." Apollos was the greatest living Old Testament scholar, and Paul the greatest living New Covenant scholar, yet Paul said they were third-level galley slaves for the sake of Christ.

(b) The contrast

In contrast, Paul indicts the proud, boastful, honor-seeking Corinthians in 1 Corinthians 4:8-13: "Now ye are full, now ye are rich, ye have reigned as kings without us; and I would to God ye did reign, that we also might reign with you. For I think that God hath set forth us, the apostles, last, as it were appointed to death; for we are made a spectacle unto the world, and to angels, and to men. We are fools for Christ's sake, but ye are wise in Christ; we are weak, but ye are strong; ye are honorable, but we are despised. Even unto this present hour we both hunger, and thirst, and are naked, and are buffeted, and have no certain dwelling place; and labor, working with our own hands. Being reviled, we bless; being persecuted, we endure it; being defamed, we entreat; we are made as the filth of the world, and are the offscouring of all things unto this day." The Corinthians didn't know what true greatness is. They were puffed up and proud. But the apostles were the ones who were truly exalted because they endured suffering for the sake of the kingdom.

Be a Servant of Servants

In his book *Spiritual Leadership*, J. Oswald Sanders quotes William Law's *Serious Call*: "Let every day be a day of humility; condescend to all the weaknesses and infirmities of your fellow-creatures, cover their frailties, love their excellencies, encourage their virtues, relieve their wants, rejoice in their prosperities, compassionate their distress, receive their friendship, overlook their unkindness, forgive their malice, be a servant of servants, and condescend to do the lowliest offices of the lowest of mankind" ([Chicago: Moody, 1980], p. 90).

Sanders also quotes Samuel Brengle, who, when he was referred to as great, wrote in his diary, "If I appear great in their eyes, the Lord is most graciously helping me to see how absolutely nothing I am without Him, and helping me to keep little in my own eyes. He does use me. But I am so concerned that He uses me and that it is not of me the work is done. The axe cannot boast of the trees that it has cut down. It could do nothing but for the woodsman. He made it, he sharpened it, and he used it. The moment he throws it aside, it becomes only old iron. O that I may never lose sight of this" (p. 90). The heart of the servant is the heart that is truly great.

b) Slavery (v. 27)

> "And whosoever will be chief [Gk., *protos*, "first"] among you, let him be your servant [Gk., *doulos*]."

Doulos is a word of even lesser nobility than *diakonos*. It means "bondslave." We don't have slaves, so it is harder for us to understand that concept. But during New Testament times people knew what it was like to see slaves whipped and beaten. *Doulos* is a graphic demonstration of how committed we should be in serving one another.

(1) Affirming the path of pain

Paul viewed himself as a slave. He knew that his life was not his own—that his Master was in charge. He said, "Whether we live, we live unto the Lord; and whether we die, we die unto the Lord; whether we live, therefore, or die, we are the Lord's" (Rom. 14:8). He was a slave that was bound to Christ. He said to the Corinthians, "Death worketh in us, but life in you. . . . For all things are for your sakes" (2 Cor. 4:12, 15). Slavishly did he fulfill his responsibility before God for the sake of others. He knew some day there would be a reward—a great weight of glory that was so much beyond his light affliction (2 Cor. 4:17). Certainly Paul did what he did because he sought to be exalted, but he also did it that the Lord might be glorified in his exaltation. That was demonstrated by his willingness to endure the path of pain.

(2) Avoiding the path of pain

I see many people who want to follow the path to glory without the pain. They build Christian organizations to insulate and exalt themselves. They experience little pain or suffering. I look at my own life and sometimes question if my own motives can remain pure. All of us need to check our motives. Paul serves as an example of one who sought the glory but who was also willing to bear the pain.

J. Oswald Sanders writes, "Scars are the authentic marks of faithful discipleship and true spiritual leadership. It was said of one leader, 'He belonged to that class of early martyrs whose passionate soul made an early holocaust of the physical man' " (*Spiritual Leadership*, p. 171).

Sanders quotes the following poem by Amy Carmichael (pp. 171-72):

Hast thou no scar?
No hidden scar on foot, or side, or hand?
I hear thee sung as mighty in the land,
I hear them hail thy bright ascendant star:
Hast thou no scar?

Hast thou no wound?
Yet, I was wounded by the archers, spent.
Leaned me against the tree to die, and rent
By ravening beasts that compassed me, I
    swooned:
Hast thou no wound?

No wound? No scar?
Yes, as the master shall the servant be,
And pierced are the feet that follow Me;
But thine are whole. Can he have followed far
Who has no wound? No scar?

The Cost of Greatness

The cost of greatness is humble, sacrificial service. I wish young Christians would understand that, especially those who go into the ministry. I pray that they would not fear the hard place but seek it that they might receive the greater weight of glory. Time is so short, and eternity is so long. The cost of greatness may be persecution or even death—in some cultures that is more likely than others. But in every culture there is a price to pay.

1. Loneliness

The true path to glory is marked by loneliness. A. W. Tozer once said, "Loneliness seems to be the one price the saint must pay for his saintliness" (cited in Warren Wiersbe's *The Best of A. W. Tozer* [Grand Rapids: Baker, 1978], p. 198). The godly person is so consumed by what God has called him to do that he loses sight of the world around him. Even the good things sometimes cannot be fully enjoyed because the man holds deep in his heart God's mandate to accomplish His goals for eternity. There is loneliness in that kind of commitment. Most people don't understand the burden to be borne in the pursuit of glory along the path of suffering.

2. Weariness

Fatigue is the price of pushing past mediocrity. I have never met a man or woman abandoned to the cause of God who wasn't tired and weary.

3. Criticism

You can expect to be misunderstood, misrepresented, misjudged, and accused. To handle that without self-defense and self-justification means to bear the burden between yourself and the Lord, and perhaps someone dear to you.

There is much pain strewn along the path to glory, but it is but momentary light affliction compared to the eternal weight of glory.

It is not wrong to seek to be first. I want to be all that God wants me to be. I want to be known as one who served Him with my whole heart. It's not wrong to seek that. But to do so means you must be a slave and give your life away. In the world, the great ones are those who can manipulate the most people, ambitiously seek self-glory, dominate others, and charm others into doing what they want done. But that's not how it is in God's kingdom. William Barclay said, "The world may assess a man's greatness by the number of people whom he controls and who are at his beck and call; or by his intellectual standing and his academic eminence; or by the number of committees of which he is a member; or by the size of his bank balance and the material possessions which he has amassed; but in the assessment of Jesus Christ these things are irrelevant" (*The Gospel of Matthew,* vol. 2 [Philadelphia: Westminster, 1975], pp. 233-34). What is relevant is a person's humility.

Ask yourself: What sacrifice do I make to serve Christ? Do I tend to demand to be served more than I offer service? If I must face something uncomfortable in the process of serving Christ, am I willing to do it? Those are important questions we all need to face every day.

B. The Example (v. 28)

1. The service of Christ (v. 28*a*)

"Even as the Son of man came not to be ministered unto [be served], but to minister [serve]."

If you say you love Christ and abide in Him, 1 John 2:6 says you ought "to walk, even as he walked." Christ's life was utterly abandoned to humble, unselfish service on behalf of others.

a) His humiliation

Philippians 2:6-8 says Jesus "thought it not robbery to be equal with God, but made himself of no reputation, and took upon him the form of a servant, and was made in the likeness of men; and being found in fashion as a man, he humbled himself and became obedient unto death, even the death of the cross." The greatest humiliation possible for God was to become a man, yet Jesus Christ did just that. The sovereign of the universe condescended to become a victim of sin. That's why Christ is the greatest in the kingdom; His was the greatest display of humility.

b) His humanity

The words *Son* and *man* in verse 28 identify Christ as our example. "Son of man" is a messianic term drawn from Daniel 7:13 and is used more than eighty times by Christ in the gospels to refer to Himself. He is the incarnate One, the Messiah—God in human flesh.

He didn't come like other kings. That's what confused Pilate, who said, "Art thou the King of the Jews?" (John 18:33). Pilate was saying, "You don't look like a king, and You sure don't act like one. You've been abused, maligned, and mistreated, yet You don't retaliate. It's obvious that You don't have any kingdom or possessions. How can You be a king?" By all worldly standards there was no way Jesus could be a king. Jesus replied that Pilate couldn't understand anything about His kingdom because it wasn't Pilate's kind of kingdom (John 18:36). Most kings demand to be served, but this King came to serve.

Jesus said, "I am among you he that serveth" (Luke 22:27). He demonstrated that when He washed the feet of the disciples. They were so self-seeking that they wouldn't even think of washing each other's feet, so the Lord took off His outer garment, put a towel around His waist, and washed theirs (John 13:4-5). He is our pattern of service.

2. The death of Christ (v. 28b-c)

   a) The ultimate service (v. 28b)

      "And to give his life."

      The ultimate act of service is to die on behalf of someone else. Jesus said, "Greater love hath no man than this, that a man lay down his life for his friends. Ye are my friends, if ye do whatever I command you" (John 15:13-14). Jesus sets the pattern for us. He gave His life on our behalf.

      The passage could have ended here, emphasizing that Jesus gave His life in service and that we must do the same. But there is more to His death than that.

130

b) The ultimate ransom (v. 28*c*)

"A ransom for many."

Here we are introduced to the redemptive work of Christ—His substitutionary, vicarious, redeeming act on the cross. True, Christ serves as an example of one who was willing to suffer for others. First Peter 2:21 makes that clear: "Christ also suffered for us, leaving us an example." But Peter also said His death was more than an example: "Who his own self bore our sins in his own body" (1 Pet. 2:24). His death was an act of ransom and redemption.

(1) Its price

The word translated "ransom" is *lutron* in the Greek text. It is only used twice in the New Testament, Mark 10:45 being the other place. *Lutron* was the price paid for the release of a slave. We were slaves of sin, Satan, the flesh, and the world. Christ paid the *lutron* to release us. Romans 8:21 says that the creation will also "be delivered from the bondage of corruption into the glorious liberty of the children of God." There was a price a slave could pay to be released, but he could never earn it because he was a slave. How could he possibly amass enough money to buy his freedom when all he received was enough to sustain the bare necessities? We could no more buy our freedom than a slave could. Someone else had to pay the price, and Christ did it by becoming the ransom.

Although the noun form of *lutron* is only used twice in the New Testament, related forms are found throughout the New Testament. The idea of ransom and redemption is common in Scripture. First Corinthians 6:20 says, "Ye are bought with a price." We have been redeemed. Peter sums this thought up wonderfully in 1 Peter 1:18-19: "Ye were not redeemed with corruptible things, like silver and gold . . . but with the precious blood of Christ, as of a lamb without blemish and without spot."

The passage comes to a wonderful climax in that Jesus is not only our example, but also our redemption.

(2) Its purpose

The word translated "for" (Gk., *anti*) in Matthew 20:28 indicates an important theological term. It means "in exchange for something" or "in the place of something." Christ is saying that He is a ransom in exchange for many. It was His death for ours, His life for ours—He bore our sin.

(3) Its participants

You may wonder why Christ said He died for "many" (v. 28). Does that mean some are outside His ability to ransom? Does it teach a limited atonement? No, "many" is simply an expression referring to all. It is used to contrast those who benefit from the sacrifice to the one who made it.

Romans 5:12 says, "Wherefore, as by one man sin entered into the world, and death by sin, and so death passed upon all men, for all have sinned." When Adam sinned, death came to all men for all have sinned. Verse 15 says, "Through the offense of one many are dead." What does the "many" refer to? All. So "many" is used to demonstrate contrast. Verse 19 says, "As by one man's disobedience many were made sinners." The same thing is true here—the "many" refers to everyone. I believe Christ provided a ransom for all. But each person needs to appropriate it for himself by faith.

Conclusion

Because of what Christ did, Philippians 2:9-11 says, "God also hath highly exalted him, and given him a name which is above every name, that at the name of Jesus every knee should bow, of things in heaven, and things in earth, and things under the earth, and that every tongue should confess that Jesus Christ is Lord, to the glory of God, the Father." Because Christ humbled Himself and offered Himself in sacrificial service to others, God highly exalted Him. His glory is in proportion to His humility. Capacity for glory in the kingdom is in direct proportion to the humble service you have rendered to others. If your spiritual life is on target, then you will seek the eternal weight of glory. That will cause you to serve Christ with a whole heart and be willing to follow the path of pain or suffering.

Focusing on the Facts

1. What characterizes the great men of the Old Testament? Give some examples (see pp. 116-18).
2. For whom is greatness in the kingdom of God reserved (see p. 118)?
3. Contrast the great men of the world with the great men of God's kingdom (see p. 119)?
4. Is it a right motivation to seek to be great in the kingdom? Explain (see pp. 120-21)?
5. What is God's path to glory (see p. 121)?
6. What original meaning did the Greek word translated "servant" or "deacon" have in New Testament times (Matt. 20:26; see p. 123)?
7. Which Greek word did the apostle Paul use to describe himself in 1 Corinthians 4:1? Describe its meaning (see p. 124).
8. What does the Greek word translated "servant" in Matthew 20:27 mean? How does it differ from the word translated "servant" in verse 26 (see p. 126)?
9. What did Paul know he would gain as a result of his service to others (2 Cor. 4:17; see p. 126)?
10. What is the cost of greatness? Describe three things that mark the path to greatness (see pp. 127-28).
11. Why can Christ be considered the greatest in God's kingdom (Phil. 2:6-8; see p. 129)?

12. What was Christ's ultimate act of service (Matt. 20:28; see p. 130)?
13. Why is Christ's death more to us than an example (1 Pet. 2:24; see pp. 130-31)?
14. Define ransom. Explain the concept of Christ as our ransom (see pp. 131-32).

Pondering the Principles

1. What sacrifices have you made recently to serve Christ? In comparison, how many times have you demanded to be served—do you desire to have your needs met first and tend to demand that your rights be considered? When you are faced with an uncomfortable task for the sake of Christ, are you willing to do it? Based on Matthew 20:26-27, what should be your attitude in every circumstance? Certainly following the path of true greatness is difficult, but every believer should make the commitment to do so—not only for his own benefit but also to give glory to God.

2. Read Philippians 2:6-8. Explain the example that Christ gave us. List each action on His part that represents humble sacrifice. Verse 5 says we ought to have the same attitude as Christ. But how can we practically follow Christ's example? Read Philippians 2:2-4. Begin to put those verses into practice today. Seek to put the interests of others before yours. As you do so, you will find yourself becoming more Christlike.

Scripture Index